A
RAHNER
HANDBOOK

Robert Kress

John Knox Press
ATLANTA

Library of Congress Cataloging in Publication Data

Kress, Robert.
    A Rahner handbook.

    Bibliography: p.
    Includes index.
    1. Rahner, Karl, 1904-   . 2. Theology,
Doctrinal—History—20th century.   3. Theology,
Catholic—History—20th century.   I. Title.
BX4705.R287K74   230′.2′0924   81-85333
ISBN 0-8042-0652-X   AACR2

© copyright John Knox Press 1982
10 9 8 7 6 5 4 3 2 1
Printed in the United States of America
John Knox Press
Atlanta, Georgia 30365

For
Raban, OSB and Basil, OSB
Karl, SJ and Colleen, ISS
in gratitude for
mystagogy
into the mystery of being:
God.
And to Patty Cox for typing this
manuscript.

Preface

I have written this book for those who want to read Karl Rahner but who may be hesitant to try. They may be afraid because others have told them they should be—Rahner is difficult. Or they may have already tried—Rahner was difficult. So they are reluctant to try again.

Is Rahner all this difficult? Yes and no. Beginning with certain of his writings will almost certainly assure failure. To prevent this I have included an appendix, "How to Read Rahner." Even some introductions are not helpful. Sometimes they simply repeat the difficult passages, which is no help, and sometimes they are more difficult than Rahner himself. I still remember some helpful advice from my own undergraduate days: "If you have trouble understanding the commentaries on St. Thomas Aquinas, try reading St. Thomas himself." It usually worked.

I have tried not to make my introduction more difficult than Rahner himself. I have also tried to keep the flavor of Rahner's theology and theologizing. Some years ago Marshall McLuhan proclaimed that the medium is the message. This applies more to some theologians than others and does apply to Rahner. Throughout this book I shall point out the intimacy between the content and the style of his thought. So that the reader might savor the flavor of Rahner's theology, I shall use his own words when this is appropriate. At other times I shall try to let Rahner clearly speak in my own words. In this manner I hope that my book will be easier than Rahner himself, but I also hope that it will not be something different from or alien to Rahner's thought. Thus it will be able to serve as a true initiation or mystagogy, as Rahner might say, into his thought.

None of this is intended, of course, to declare Karl Rahner a saint. I gladly remand his canonization to the proper authorities—history and the church. Rahner himself is also quite aware that one can be a fine, upstanding human and Christian without having read one word of his. (Even an admirer like me knows that.)

But I also know that ignorance of Rahner's thought on the part of those capable of understanding it is an impoverishment. I have written this book primarily as an introduction and throughout have kept the needs of beginners in mind. However, I have also written this book as a theologian. I hope that it will be of interest to those who are not beginners. The time allowed to prepare the final version has enabled me to use the latest volumes of Rahner's collected writings which are not yet translated. For various reasons I have generally preferred to make my own translations.

Karl Rahner has always seemed to me to try not to come between his hearers or readers and the truth he was explaining. As writer and teacher he has truly been a mediator. I hope that my little book will also be a mediator—between its readers and Rahner's theology. And thus it can also be a mediator to Christ Jesus, "the one mediator between God and mankind . . . God our saviour [who] wants everyone to be saved and reach full knowledge of the truth" (1 Timothy 2:4-6).

Contents

CHAPTER 1

Life and Work

Karl Rahner was born March 5, 1904 in Freiburg, Germany. Of seven children, as his brother and fellow Jesuit Hugo remarks, Karl was the oldest of the youngest and Hugo the youngest of the oldest. Both brothers grew up in a traditionally pious Catholic family in predominantly Catholic southern Germany. Their father was a teacher in the local high school and their mother a typical German housewife and mother, who lived to be one hundred years old. Rahner himself speaks of her as the valiant woman of the biblical wisdom (Proverbs 31:10-31; Sirach 26:1-4). Karl and Hugo attended the same church and the same schools. Karl admits that his performance was good, but thoroughly average.

Three years after Hugo, and rather to everyone's surprise, Karl also entered the religious order of the Society of Jesus. He was, as Hugo notes, quick to point out that his choice was in no wise influenced by his older brother's earlier entry. For Rahner's own life, theology and spirituality, the importance of this order and its founder, St. Ignatius of Loyola, cannot be exaggerated. This will be developed later on. However, in a book about Karl Rahner, Jesuit and Ignatian must be present from the very beginning.

Since his days as a novice (1922-1924) in Feldkirch, Austria, Karl Rahner has been a dedicated and loyal Jesuit, with an enormous capacity for work. Not that he is drudge and drone. His lectures and writings as well as his personal life indicate that he quite enjoys a glass of wine, a mouth-watering Schnitzel, a good cup of coffee—frequent metaphors in the Rahnerian vocabulary. Nevertheless, theology has been his life. Seldom has the coinciding of office and person, an often recurring theme in his theology, been more striking than in Karl Rahner. Mystic and believer, priest and professor, he has lived his theological career with the single-minded intensity appropriate for a follower of Christ and a devotee of St. Ignatius of Loyola.

On April 27, 1924, he took his first vows as a Jesuit. He followed the usual academic course of Jesuit training, one year of philosophy at Feldkirch and two more at Pullach, near Munich. During these years Rahner devoted special effort to the study of Immanuel Kant and the Belgian Jesuit, Joseph Marechal, who had attempted to reconcile the philosophies of Kant and Aquinas. Rahner spent his regency, a two- to three-year period of practical experience and work, as a Latin teacher in Feldkirch. In 1929, he went to Valkenburg, Holland, for his theological studies. After his priestly ordination in Munich (July 26, 1932), he completed his final year of theology and then spent his year of tertianship (a year long period of retreat and reflection) at St. Andra in Austria.

In 1934, his Jesuit superiors, intending him to teach the history of philosophy, sent him to Freiburg to do his doctorate in philosophy. There and then his life's journey, so apparently peaceful if not prosaic so far, received its first jolt. At the University of Freiburg, the chair for Catholic philosophy was occupied by a certain Martin Honegger. Herbert Vorgrimler describes him as "a naive, narrow-minded representative of that rationalistic neo-scholasticism which had little more to do with St. Thomas Aquinas."[1] His best claim to fame is that he rejected Karl Rahner's doctoral dissertation, thereby depriving him of his doctorate in philosophy. However, the Freiburg years were by no means a total loss. The featured philosopher there was Martin Heidegger, whose highly restricted seminars Rahner was able to attend. At Freiburg Rahner was also in the company of Gustave Siewerth, Bernard Welte, Max Muller, John Baptist Lotz and others. All of these went on to become well-known philosophers in their own right. Although they were never formally organized, they do merit the title conferred on them by Erich Przywara, namely "The Catholic Heidegger School." They attempted to rejuvenate the Catholic philosophical tradition on the basis of certain insights inspired by Heidegger. They focused on a reinterpretation of St. Thomas Aquinas. As Herbert Vorgrimler noted, this meant that their philosophizing was in stark contrast to the semi-official scholasticism of the standard textbooks used in Catholic schools and seminaries.

A good example of this "Catholic Heidegger School's" approach is provided by Rahner's dissertation, later published as *Spirit in the*

World. He had not intended it to be merely a historical exposition of St. Thomas' text, but a real philosophical work inspired by St. Thomas' insights. "The concern of the book is not the critique of knowledge, but the metaphysics of knowledge, a theme from the center of the Thomistic metaphysics of knowledge. . . . An interpretation of St. Thomas is at work here which has its origin in modern philosophy." Rahner "hoped [to] receive the favor of a judgment which shares the objective concerns of contemporary philosophy, and which joins Thomas in looking first at the matter itself, and only then at the formulation which it found in Thomas."[2] We all know that his hope was vain. Honegger found too much modern, not enough Thomas in his evaluation, which Vorgrimler terms "inept." He gives some appalling examples. It is to Rahner's credit, and probably a reflection of the "indifference" of his Jesuit spirituality (a certain equanimity of mind in the face of good and evil) that he has not complained about this travesty.

Theological Beginnings

In 1936 Rahner returned to Innsbruck where he completed his theological doctorate. His dissertation was on the birth of the church from the pierced side of Christ according to the patristic interpretation of John 19:34. Since he had already published several other scholarly studies in German and French on Origen, Bonaventure, and Evagrius Ponticus, Rahner was officially appointed to the theology faculty of the University of Innsbruck as Privatdozent on July 1, 1937. As Rahner himself remarks, it was not precisely because he had not received his philosophy doctorate, but because a theology professor was needed, and because "my religious superiors were of the opinion that I wouldn't do it any worse than many others" (XII, 599).[3] He began his teaching career at Innsbruck. Philosophy's failure, according to Honegger, was now on his way to becoming theology's "trailblazer," as Marquette University described Rahner in conferring upon him the Pere Marquette Discovery Medal in 1979.

His experience at Freiburg did not sour Rahner on philosophy. Throughout his career he has had an "almost superstitious respect for philosophy" (XII, 599). It is not surprising, then, that in the summer of 1937 he gave a series of lectures at the famous Salzburg Summer

School of Theology on the "Foundations of a Philosophy of Religion." These lectures continued the inquiry begun in his dissertation at Freiburg and laid the foundation for his other major "philosophical" work, *Hearers of the Word*, which first appeared in 1941.

What can be called the kernel of Rahner's thought is already present in these two philosophical studies. It is especially evident in his first published book, on prayer, titled *Encounters with Silence*. The difficulties of translating Rahner are also revealed immediately. In this first book he already demonstrates his linguistic ability—not disability, as many would like to assert. He explicitly expresses the enduring heart of all his theology with a play on words not easily translated. "You have seized (*ergriffen*) me. I have not comprehended (*begriffen*) you. You have transformed my being in its very root and origin. You have made me a sharer in your life and being."[4] This is the point from which he always begins and to which he always returns. This circle is described by various authors as being grounded in "God's communication of himself to man" or "the experience of grace" or "the human being as mystery," that is, as "open directedness to God."[5] Ignatian Mysticism—the everyday experience of God, finding God in all things, being always open to the always greater God—has certainly influenced the mode and content of all Rahner's theology and philosophy. It is crucially important to understand at the very beginning that grace, not philosophy, is the beginning and the heart of Rahner's theology. This statement is deliberately ambiguous. In it the word *grace* can mean both the reality and the theological treatment of the reality. In both senses grace is the beginning and heart of Rahner's theology. Thus the title of an interview on his seventieth birthday is most apt. It sums up his theology and his life: "Grace as the Center and Heart of Human Existence."[6] The theology of grace was one of Rahner's specialties at Innsbruck. By 1956 his mimeographed notes had gone through four revisions and attained a volume of 350 single-spaced typed pages.

However, Rahner's life and theology of grace was not purely academic. From the very beginning of his teaching career Rahner has had to contend with extremes in his church: from the right those who regard everything except the incantation of past formulae as heresy; from the left those who evoke not diversity and variety, but hostility and division. Already in 1938 Rahner had joined forces with theologians and other scholars to search for ways to allow greater creativity within his church. Those who were surprised by the vigor of Rahner's response in 1979 when his former student, J. B. Metz, was refused a theological chair at Munich should recall those earlier repressive ecclesiastical conditions. It is obvious that Rahner, who himself suffered from them, fears that they are again in the ascendancy.[7]

In any case, Rahner's 1938 efforts were to bear fruit only later. A much greater oppression had arisen. Soon all were to be engulfed in the grim night of Nazism. Shortly after the Nazi *Anschluss* of Austria, the theology faculty of the University of Innsbruck was suppressed (July 1938). The Jesuits continued to conduct classes in their own residence until October 1939, when that was also suppressed by the Nazis. Some of the Innsbruck Jesuits, including Karl's brother, Hugo, went to Switzerland to continue their theological and seminary mission in exile. Karl Rahner remained in Austria, where he had made his final vows as a Jesuit on August 15, 1939. Officially forbidden by the Nazis to stay in Tyrol, Rahner was invited by the Archibishop of Vienna to work in the Diocesan Pastoral Institute there and to continue his teaching as best he could under the circumstances. During the war years he also left the comparative safety of Vienna to lecture in such cities as Leipzig, Dresden, Strasbourg and Cologne. In the summer of 1944 Vienna became the victim of increased Gestapo terror. All public activity became less and less possible. Rahner left the city for rural Bavaria where he did parochial work until August of 1945, when he was called to the Jesuit College in Pullach to teach theology. During these "years of misery" he also did considerable social and pastoral work in the bombed city of Munich. His 1946 Lenten Lectures in St. Michael's Church "On the Need and Blessing of Prayer" were published two years later and are regarded by many as a modern spiritual classic.

Teaching

In 1949, he was able to resume his professorship at Innsbruck. In a three-year cycle of dogmatic and systematic theology, his specialties were (1) creation and elevation of humanity, original sin; (2) justification, grace, theological virtues; (3) sacraments of penance, holy orders, and anointing of the sick. In addition to these major courses he also conducted seminars on a wide range of topics. During his Innsbruck years a real treat for his students was the so-called Free Theological Colloquy. On Friday evenings after supper Rahner and whoever wished to come would assemble in a classroom. He would accept any and all questions from the audience and then think aloud for two hours.

During these years Rahner's activity was prodigious. As conditions in postwar Germany and Europe improved, and as Rahner's fame increased, he was called upon to lecture almost everywhere to almost everyone about almost everything. Especially pleasing to Rahner were the retreats and recollections he could fit into his busy schedule and, perhaps above all, the First Mass Sermons he was invited to preach by his former students. He was, and is, according to his own words, above all else a believer and priest. Such occasions reminded us, and Rahner himself, I suspect, that he was not only a theologian but also a human being.

I well remember the First Mass of my classmate, Franz Graef, in Heidelberg. Rahner not only preached but also played with Klaus and Monika (Franz's little brother and sister) and their toys. He also played with us and our more grown up "toys," obviously relishing Vater Graef's wine and Mutter Graef's food, defending the fittingness (*convenientia* in the scholastic theological terminology so familiar to him) of the artistic binding of Franz's breviary (prayer books) which his sister Hildegard had done in colors corresponding to the liturgical seasons.

For all his brilliance (in spite of his frequent self-deprecations, Rahner knows that he is brilliant), he is not pompous and pretentious. And for all his commitment to the priesthood, celibacy, and theology, Rahner is certainly a refutation of the suspicion that people so committed must be dull and distracted, withdrawn from and hostile to the joys of everyday life. During a 1979 visit to Louisville, Kentucky, Rahner was scheduled to visit a thoroughbred horse farm, the Oxmoor shopping center, and a church. Shortness of time forced a selection, so the church freely ceded to the shopping center. Department stores, especially their toy departments, have always fascinated Karl Rahner. On the following day, officially proclaimed "Karl

Rahner Day in Louisville," he was promoted to the rank of Kentucky Colonel and Captain of the Belle of Louisville Riverboat, *honoris causa.* For him "Finding God in All Things" is not only a principle of Ignatian mysticism but is also an experience of daily life.

An intense lecturer, Rahner packed the lecture halls at Innsbruck, where I was graced to hear him from 1954-1958. His style was and still is his own. It is not without its difficulties, but it is more than adequately rewarding to those willing to make the effort it requires. Seldom was there the scuffing of shoes on the classroom floor—the traditional sign of student disapproval. The annual exception occurred when Rahner would make his gesture to the pontifical status of the theological faculty and lecture in Latin instead of German. Fortunately, this linguistic detour was always brief. In contrast to some lecturers whose efforts at clarity were so clear that, when the proof was explained, one had not yet perceived the problem, Rahner's style emphasized the status of the question, the problematic, both historical and doctrinal. How often did we hear what was both Rahnerian self-defense and methodological principle: "Das Klarere ist nicht immer das Wahrere" (The more clear is not always necessarily the more true.)? Rahner's approach enabled careful listeners to gain not only knowledge but also insight.

Rahner is anything but a dull lecturer. Not unlike a preoccupied bear tracing and retracing his steps, Rahner paced back and forth on the elevated room-wide platform before 250 and more students, thinking his theological thoughts aloud in a deep, rumbling voice. Hearing Rahner ruminating on the fragility of contingent being and the prolixity of death on dark days deep in the narrow Alpine valley at Innsbruck, one could indeed experience the meaning of *memento mori*: "Remember, O man, that thou art dust and to dust thou shalt return." His lectures, however, were also filled with witty and arty turns of phrases as well as homey and earthy metaphors. In the fitting contexts, Rahner could refer to the prevalent textbook theology as "Wald und Wiesen Theologie" (theology of the woods and meadows) or "landläufige" (which, on his lips, evoked the connotations of a thoroughly dull and unexciting landscape). Of his religious order kinsmen, he could remark that they had always been good merchants. Of his own Jesuit traditional piety, he did not hesitate to remark that the celebration of the Eucharist was the preparation of the host for the evening benediction. During his days under siege by Roman and other authorities, he could still jest that, like Peter Olivi in an earlier age, he had indeed been aimed at by his detractors, but their big cannons had missed. Unplanned, these and other bon mots seemed to catch Rahner himself by surprise. He would suddenly stop his pacing, look up, grin and laugh aloud, partly at himself and partly with us. The general importance of his oral style to the method and content of his thought has been pointed out.[8]

His writings are also replete with sarcastic observations. He introduces some considerations on variations in the practice of the sacrament of penance by remarking that "St. Joseph did not, after all, make the first confessional." Also, "How afraid one is when, because there's nothing else to do, one tunes in the 'Catholic Morning Devotional' on television, wondering what in the world will happen this time! Indeed, one is relieved and happy when the priest is not obese and has clean fingernails." Theologians, of course, are not spared, and, above all, not Rahner himself. In "Dialogue on Sleep, Prayer and Other Things" between a doctor and pastor, Rahner has the former assert that "I have always thought that theologians do most for sleep through their lectures and writings." After disclaiming that a particular article is philosophical, Rahner continues that "it will, nevertheless, also reveal that even in theology one must also think" (III, 228, 421, 264; VI, 185).

During these Innsbruck years Rahner, like other creative Catholic theologians, suffered from censorious church policies. Rahner escaped the immediate fallout of the encyclical *Humani Generis* (1950). However, by 1962 he was under Roman pre-censorship. This meant that he could not publish or publicly lecture without prior permission from the proper ecclesiastical superiors. The date is interesting—three years after Pope John XXIII had announced the Second Vatican Council and the very year it was to open. The siege mentality forces in the church would have been pleased to exclude Rahner from the Council and to nullify his influence generally. But they were not to succeed. From Germany the Paulus-Gesellschaft sent the Pope a protest and petition with the signatures of 250 prominent political and academic persons (among them Konrad Adenauer) asking that the restrictive order be rescinded. At this time Rahner gave one of his most impassioned addresses at the Austrian Katholikentag (June 1, 1962) on the text from 1 Thessalonians 5:19, "Do Not Extinguish the Spirit." Although conditioned by the particular situation of the church then, this address still deserves periodic perusal. It is in Volume VII of *Theological Investigations*. The fascist spirit which strives, whether from the right or the left, to suppress the Spirit has not vanished entirely from the church. Apparently it never will.

Rahner was chosen as a *peritus* (expert) for the Council by Cardinal König of Vienna and also served as an advisor to Cardinal Döpfner. Thus the censorship order lost its practical force. Finally, he was also chosen by Pope John to be one of the 195 council experts. Henceforth he had access to the council commissions and plenary sessions. In his customary self-deprecating manner, Rahner makes light of his contribution to and influence on Vatican II. But it was enormous. With other theologians like Yves Congar, Edward Schillebeeckx, and Joseph Ratzinger, he was able to rescue the Council from the preparatory commissions' restrictive approach and content. These have been described variously as narrow, defensive, condemnatory, and triumphalist. A German friend and colleague from Innsbruck once remarked, not without humor of course, "Wouldn't it be something if the Council were to canonize Rahner's theology!" An exaggeration, of course, but not without its own appeal. However appealing, though, it would violate Rahner's own pleas for tolerance and pluralism in the church in general and in theology in particular.

A negative evaluation of Rahner's influence, which nonetheless indicates how great it was, is offered by Ralph Wiltgen. In his evaluative history of Vatican II, Wiltgen asserts that the Council was dominated by the Germans, who themselves were under the hegemony of Karl Rahner. He asserts that in one critical debate "Fr. Rahner—and the European Alliance—had won by a margin of 17 votes," and thus "The Rhine had begun to flow into the Tiber."[9] A well-known American theologian refused to shake hands with Rahner during the latter's first trip to the United States on the grounds that he was a modernist heretic. However, such gestures tell us more about the ones making them than they do about Rahner. They remain only negative ciphers, pointing to Rahner's influence and reputation which were firmly secured by his presence and efficacy at Vatican II.

At this time he left Innsbruck, where, one hears, he had not always escaped the suspicions and, perhaps, envies of his confreres. In 1964 the University of Munich appointed him to succeed Romano Guardini as *Professor für Christliche Weltanschauung und Religionsphilosophie.* Although this is one of the most prestigious university chairs in Germany, it had one significant drawback. Since it was in the Philosophy Faculty, Rahner could not direct doctoral candidates and dissertations in theology. In 1967 he responded to an extraordinary call and went to the University of Münster to take the chair for dogmatic theology in the Catholic theological faculty.

He remained there until his retirement in 1971 when he returned to Munich. His retirement has meant only that he is now professor emeritus, not that he has ceased working. He still lectures and writes. In his "retirement" he was finally able to complete and publish his long promised and awaited "systematic theology," *Foundations of Christian Faith* (1976, German; 1978, American). Even this has not really retired Rahner. He is true to his own dictum, "One should never stop thinking too early." Even on his seventy-fifth birthday he was still fascinated by the need for a reinterpretation of the much-maligned doctrine of apocatastasis, which asserts that in the end everyone will be saved, none condemned. "Realist" that he is though, he wondered "whether my time and strength may be sufficient anymore."[10]

The years after Vatican II have brought him both the scholarly and hierarchical recognition earlier denied him. Pope John's high praise of Rahner has been reported. Pope Paul VI encouraged Rahner to continue courageously along the path Rahner himself had blazed.[11] In 1979 Rahner's trailblazing contribution was explicitly acknowledged. He was given Marquette University's "Pere Marquette Discovery Award," presented only once before, to the crew of Apollo II. "The person who receives the medal must have accomplished a breakthrough which may be considered a discovery in some field of human knowledge or in some sphere which adds to the advancement of man." This description of the medal is also a description of the man and theologian to whom it was presented. In 1969 he was appointed to the International Theological Commission, at that time a recognition of not only his ability and merit, but also of his orthodoxy.

Writing

In addition to his teaching and lecturing, Rahner has been able to wage his own "Papierkrieg" or paper war. His publishing activity has been twofold, original writing and editorial. He describes the latter as "Schreckliche Kärrnerarbeit." This means something like the "numbing brute labor of a pack mule."[12] He edited and expanded Denzinger's *Enchiridion*, a collection of official doctrinal texts from the earliest creeds to present magisterial decisions, through editions 28 to 35. He also edited a greatly modified German version, which appeared in English under the title *The Church Teaches*. In 1961 he and one of his students, Vorgrimler, wrote *A Concise Theological Dictionary*, which can be regarded as a compendium of Rahner's theological approach and insights. His chief editorial work has clearly been the second, thoroughly revised edition of *Lexikon für Theologie und Kirche*, which he edited with Joseph Höfer. It consists of ten volumes of about 1,340 columns each, covering just about every topic which could be considered from a theological point-of-view. Of the 30,000 articles, Rahner himself wrote about 135. At this time Rahner resumed his earlier idea of a series of monographs on controversial topics in theology. Thus was born the series *Questiones Disputatae*, which he edited with Heinrich Schlier. Along with Franz Xavier Arnold, Viktor Schurr, and Leonhard M. Weber, Rahner edited the four-volume *Handbuch der Pastoral-theologie* (1964-1969). Of course, the basic outline for this handbook of not only individual but ecclesial pastoral theology was the work of Karl Rahner. His pastoral interests were apparent at an early date. Already in 1959 he had been able to publish a 561-page collection of his previously published articles on pastoral and practical theology, *Sendung und Gnade*, only partially translated into English. The six volumes of *Sacramentum Mundi* were intended to be a more kerygmatic and pastoral theological encyclopedia. Now out of print, it has been replaced by the one-volume *Encyclopedia of Theology*, subtitled "The Concise Sacramentum Mundi." These, again, have been edited by Karl Rahner. He was also actively involved in the establishment of *Concilium* in 1964, an international journal which was intended to further the theological developments of Vatican II. In 1968, along with Vorgrimler, his untiring collaborator in so many of these ventures, Rahner inaugurated the short-lived *Internationale Dialog Zeitschrift* to provide a forum for the Christian-Marxist dialogue which then looked so promising. It was revived in 1978. In 1980 my mail brought an advertisement from Germany for a thirty-volume encyclopedia, *Christian Faith in Modern Society*. Of course, one of the editors is Karl Rahner.

Original Writings

Rahner's most important contribution to theology has not been his editing but his original writing. In fact, his biography can be traced in his *Schriften zur Theologie* as well as in any chronicle. There are now fourteen volumes of these collected writings, totalling almost 7,500 pages. Karl Rahner has been a theologian intensely involved in the practical, concrete life of the church, responding to its immediate needs as they arise. Somewhere along the line (Karl Lehmann suggests no later than his agreement to edit the *Lexikon*), he had to make a decision that he would not be the great Catholic systematician of this age, that he would not write the comprehensive Catholic dogma text.[13] Rahner himself says, "Consequently, not much in the way of systematics could be produced," and explicitly refers to his preoccupation with "the answers to the many individual questions which my responsibility to the man of today required of me, so that he might be soberly critical and a Christian at the same time."[14] That is the self-declared purpose of all Rahner's theology—even so heavy an enterprise as the *Lexikon*. For Rahner theological understanding is not to be the privileged private possession of an intellectual elite but is to be made available to as many as possible. Because of this concern, Rahner's *Theological Investigations* are not only theological but are also autobiographical.

The publication of such a collection of previously published journal articles was first suggested by Richard Gutzwiller, a fellow Jesuit and friend of Rahner's, a university chaplain in Zurich as well as a visiting professor in Innsbruck. Several German publishers rejected the proposal, on the grounds that "such heavy stuff would never sell."[15] However, Oscar Bettschart, the director of Benziger Publishers in Einsiedeln, had independently come to the same conclusion: that Rahner's journal articles should be collected and published in book form. Together they planned to publish two volumes. However, the first grew so rapidly that it became Volumes I and II, and the originally planned second volume became III (1954-1956). The first two contained more traditionally dogmatic and systematic articles, as the subtitles indicate: "God, Christ, Mary and Grace" and "Man in the Church." The third volume is subtitled "Toward a Theology of the Spiritual Life." Their purpose Rahner himself explains (I, 8):

> The presumptuous intention of this modest collection of theological studies will be achieved if they help just a little (before they are finally forgotten) to confirm young theologians in the conviction that Catholic theology has no reason to rest on its laurels, fine though those may be, that on the contrary it can and must advance, and in such a way that it remains true to its own laws and its tradition.

The success of the first three volumes was judged "sufficient justification for this new collection" (1960), Volume IV. It is quite different from I–III, for it contains articles written between 1958-1960. Those contained in I–III were written over a much longer period of time. I think it is fair to say that IV is the purest and best single volume of dogmatic theology in the entire collection.

Volume V had a more interesting genesis, coming as it did in the censorship period. Since there was some fear that the precensorship order might prevent its publication, the editing and printing of this volume were done with great haste. Its contents (1960-1962) clearly mirror the concerns of the Second Vatican Council. Its dedication to the Paulus-Gesellschaft, which had supported Rahner during his censorship struggle, clearly mirrors the times. Volumes VI (1965) and VIII (1967, the year Rahner moved to Münster) reflect his activity at the Council: the theological discussions and the growing dialogue with secular humanist, Marxist, and futurist interpretations of the world. In between (1966) Volume VII had appeared, like III a collection of "spiritual writings" from a period of fifteen years. In the same year there also appeared another collection of spiritual writings. Its title, perhaps more than other, captures the spirit of Rahner's faith and theology: *Glaube der die Erde liebt: Christliche Besinnung im*

Alltag der Welt (Faith Which Loves the Earth: Christian Meditation in the Daily Life of the World.) Such collections of "spiritual writings" have appeared regularly during Rahner's career. He clearly regards them to be of critical importance, not only for piety, but also for theology: "In this manner of thinking, certain essential things can perhaps be intimated, which in the customary technical theological language are barely said, or are forgotten, or cannot be formulated with sufficient clarity and precision" (VII, 7). "Several smaller and larger 'pious' books are just as important to me as those which claim to be theological works" ("Selbstporträt," 21).

Volume IX contains the articles which had appeared between 1968-1970 and was aptly subtitled *Confrontations*, continuing the later themes of VIII (1965-1967). His reaction to the encyclical about artificial contraception appeared in six translations, all within 1968, the year of the original German publication. It is contained in Volume IX and remains one of the severest indictments of the kind of theologizing represented in the encyclical. Volume X appeared in 1972, containing chiefly articles which had appeared since IX, but also some earlier ones. Its subtitle is "In Dialogue with the Future." The future is of the church and of the church in and with the world. In this volume the nature and task of theology in the contemporary age return as a major concern. Rahner again feels compelled to warn that even ten volumes of *Investigations* do not a *Systematic Dogmatic Theology* make—if, indeed, theology in the contemporary situation can be written systematically at all! Even at this time, however, Rahner was at work on what has been called his summa, *Foundations of Christian Faith*. We shall briefly examine this work later on.

At long last, the volume (XI) containing Rahner's early patristic studies on the history of the sacrament of penance appeared in 1973. These studies on Scripture, the Apostolic Fathers, Montanism, Hermas, Irenaeus, Tertullian, Cyprian, the Didascalia Apostolorum, and Origen "have been brought up to date, but appear to have lost none of their original validity, since research into the sacrament of penance has not progressed much in the last two decades." These studies are of not only theoretical, but also practical value, as all of Rahner's theology. He quite correctly understands that problems in the present practice of the sacrament of penance can be solved only insofar as the past practice of the church is understood.

There was also a further, indeed, an apologetic purpose, for publishing these historical studies. Although it is impossible for me to understand how anyone even vaguely familiar with Rahner's academic history and work could make such accusations concerning his theology (among academics envy may indeed be stronger than lust), Rahner perceives that

> With not a few people I have come under the suspicion of being merely a theological speculator, who simply, with no regard for the historical reality, fires away with his theories, and who, under certain circumstances attempts to resolve the difficulties in magisterial documents through a merely speculative interpretation of such statements. . . . It clearly remains the free choice of the theologian if, in this or that individual limited investigation, he chooses to be more "historical" or "speculative." Perhaps this volume can allay the suspicion that I have no understanding of and for historical theology (XI, 11, 12).

In June, 1975, Rahner was able to dedicate Volume XII to his mother on her one hundredth birthday. Subtitled "Theology of the Experience of the Spirit," this volume ranges over a wide variety of topics. There is, however, a certain concentration on the theme that has been of "decisive importance for the author's entire theological enterprise." We briefly mentioned this theme earlier, as the starting point and heart of all of Rahner's theology. It is

> that entirely specific experience [of the Spirit] to which Ignatius of Loyola wanted to direct and lead [people] through his Spiritual Exercises. In such an experience, however, there is an inherent dynamism to mature into theological reflection, which is able to unfold more clearly and deeply that which has been immediately experienced.

And here is also Rahner's explicit confession that his

> own theologizing arose in the experience of the Ignatian Exercises and has taken shape in the light provided by the understanding and insight that there is such an efficacy of the Spirit (XII, 8, 11).

Volumes XIII and XIV were coordinated to appear in 1978 and 1979. The former contains more dogmatic and systematic articles, the latter more pastoral and spiritual. In "God and Revelation," the subtitle of XIII, classical Rahnerian concerns return: history and development of dogma, Jesus, Mary, and justification in both Roman Catholic and ecumenical contexts. In the foreword, Rahner notes that after so many volumes of collected writings he may be the subject of two expectations: a systematic summary and an explicit dialogue with those theologians who have commented on his theology. He responds that, although his *Foundations* was not intended to be such a summary, it may nevertheless be able to serve as such, and thus fulfill the first expectation. The second, however, will have to remain unsatisfied, for "my physical strength no longer seems capable of such a task" (XIII, 8).

Of Volume XIV Rahner says: "The purchaser may be at ease. In all likelihood there will be no further addition to these volumes. There are now almost 7,500 pages. That seems to me to be enough—for me and the reader" (XIV, 7). It is worth noting that he did say "in all likelihood," which is by no means an absolute promise. And given his "Concern for the Church," as this volume is entitled, it is not at all unthinkable that there might be another volume. In the foreword Rahner explicitly refers the title to the current climate of the church and theology which he does not find entirely encouraging. In the same spirit, the first chapter is entitled "About the Courage Required to Be a Christian and Remain in the Church." Throughout the entire volume Rahner is concerned to show that it is possible to be a believer and a member of the visible church, in spite of the difficulties presented by a secularized world and a sinful church. He emphasizes that the spirituality of the future must emphasize the immediate experience of God. This immediate experience does not eliminate the social, historical tradition of Jesus known as the church; they should mutually support one another. In particular Rahner intercedes in favor of the ordination of women to the priesthood. Rahner's continuing apologetic concern is indicated in a special chapter, "Why Does God Allow Us to Suffer?"

The most significant chapters are on the significance of Vatican II. Rahner suggests that the church has entered a new epoch. It has become truly a worldwide church. The transition to this third epoch of church history is as important as the transition from the first to the second, namely from Jewish Christianity to Western, hellenistic Christendom. Just as all the problems and prospects associated with

"St. Paul's Gentile Universalization" were not apparent then, neither are all the problems and prospects of the new "Universalization" now. What is undeniably clear is that this universal church can no longer be primarily Roman and Western. In the future it may not even be predominantly so. Although Rahner is writing directly for his own Roman Catholic Church, he does not deem his prognosis to be limited to it. This worldwide prospect makes all the more urgent the effective combination of the immediate experience of God in daily human life with loyal but critical church membership. Rahner has come full circle—from the Ignatian experience of the Spirit and reflection on that experience to his theology's central and most persistent idea, which is "this experience (of God, the Holy Spirit). Although it occurs in an infinite variety of forms and shapes, according to each one's own particular personal and individual nature and history, it is made by everyone" (XII, 2). Human, Christian, and churchly life all have one inner dynamism and one final goal. Rahner sums this up in a chapter titled "Eternity Through and from Time."

Systematic

There is a unity in Rahner's writings, as many and varied as they are. In spite of Rahner's protestations, and apart from the late *Foundations*, his theology is also systematic. The perceptive judgment of Karl G. Steck is certainly right on target.

> From the outside Rahner's writings appear to be very diffuse. ... However, these writings also have a substantial inner unity, which could not be greater in a theological manual, which Rahner has obviously deliberately chosen not to write. This substantial inner unity is, in my view, an advantage of Rahner's writings and not to be ignored because of his "Gehen mit der Zeit"—that is, his response to the daily needs of the Church.[16]

One can legitimately wonder about the source of such a *theological* unity in the writings of someone so attuned to the needs of the church, so committed to answering the questions of modern life. Likewise, one can wonder about the source of that *personal* unity and equanimity which has been Rahner's in a time of such ecclesial and civil tumult. In a birthday interview, he was able to describe the seventy-five years of his human life and the fifty-six years of his Jesuit life as "quite regular . . . relatively homogeneous . . . characterized by a certain monotony. . . ."

The source? Rahner at least hints at it when he describes it as "a regularity, a homogeneity that comes from a person's turning toward the final theme of theology, of religious life and also of human life in general—which comes from the one, silent, absolute but always present reality of God."[17]

More specifically, the roots of this unity may be found in two basic, mutually reinforcing principles of Ignatian Spirituality, "Finding God in All Things" and "Indifference." The latter is not to be confused with cold, apathetic not caring one way or the other. It is not the product of boredom, in which nothing is interesting or valuable. Strangely enough, this "Indifference" is the product of an "Enthusiasm" by virtue of which everything is interesting. Here enthusiasm can be taken etymologically. It means being in God, having a God within, having been seized by God. Rahner's Ignatian theology and spirituality emphasize this. It means that the kingdom of God has so overwhelmed one that one is ready and willing to do *whatever* this kingdom demands at any given time in any given place. As Hugo Rahner once explained, this kingdom often demands that one dine on thin gruel and dry bread. But at times it can equally demand that one dine on caviar and fine champagne. The readiness to dine either way precisely because of the kingdom's perceived demands—this is the true meaning of Jesuit "Indifference."

Of course this "Indifference" is only possible because of the equally Ignatian principle that God is able to be found in all things. Mystical moments have their particular and precious value. But the ordinary, day-to-day events of everyday life are equally able to mediate the experience of God. God is truly unrestricted Grace. Therefore God is the one "in whom we live, and move and have our being" (Acts 17:28). This unrestricted "nearness of God" to us enables us to "find God in all things." This, in turn, enables us to be "indifferent," for every vocation is God-given, all being is God-revealing.

It is this theology and spirituality—for Rahner the two really are one and the same—which he has taught and lived. Rahner's stated desire is "to be a human being, a Christian and, as well as I can, a priest of the church. Perhaps a theologian can't really desire anything else."[18]

CHAPTER 2

Thought

As we have seen, Rahner's entire career as a philosopher and theologian has had a strong pastoral dimension. For him,

> Theology as a whole has ultimately no other purpose than to consider how the Gospel can be preached in such a way that it both awakens and evokes belief. Theology is the necessary presupposition for the credible proclamation of the Gospel in a future which has already begun, a future of scholarly and investigative and scientific knowledge, of technology and cybernetics, of a worldwide society of humanity (X, 501, 502).

In answer to the question, "Can we say that the primary end of theology is contemplation of the truth," Rahner replied, "No. The salvation of man is the primary end."[1]

For Rahner there cannot be two theologies: one academic and scholarly, with the truth of God's divinity as its formal object; the other kerygmatic, with its own formal object, Christ as the preachable good. No, *all* theology must be salvation-theology. A theology which would be only "theoretical" and therefore uncommitted is neither permissible nor possible. "In reality, and over the long haul, that theology is most kerygmatic (preachable) which is most strictly and passionately devoted to the matter of theology itself and which is always ready to pursue its questions with increased energy" (I, 16).

Many of us think that Rahner's theology, which is certainly demanding, passionate, and relentlessly questioning, is the best proof of his own contention. The purpose of these pages is to provide an introduction to this theologian's efforts to assist all modern human beings who want to believe. According to Rahner, even "farmers digging potatoes" cannot escape the philosophical question. They too must face, positively or negatively, the question which their very existence poses and is. They too must either believe—or not believe. It is with the *Glaubensnot* of the "person in the street" with which Rahner's theology is concerned. Whoever overlooks this automatically misappreciates Rahner's theology.

Faith and Culture

One German word can often supply a whole sentence, if not paragraph. And that is the case with *Glaubensnot*. It means belief's or faith's need. It also connotes the distress of those who wish and need to believe. This need has two dimensions, which can be called the cultural and the philosophical (ontological). Although these two dimensions can be distinguished and reflected on separately, they are not really separate but always exist in one another. The cultural dimension is more easily perceived. It varies from age to age and place to place. It is the particular form that the philosophical dimension takes in any particular here and now. All people have the same philosophical *Glaubensnot*, but the particular way any one of us experiences this need is different because each of us lives in a different culture.

Culturally, our belief must deal with today's society. It has been described as empiricist, positivist, secularist, sensate, scientific. Such culture makes it especially difficult to understand that anything exists beyond that which is immediately sensed—seen, heard, felt. Rahner frequently notes that this contemporary need of faith is intensified because it comes immediately after a period in which society had provided so much cultural support for the Christian faith that it seemed almost natural, automatic, and spontaneous to be a Christian. How could one not believe! It was all so clear: Church, Christ, God! Here Rahner's own cultural experience is clearly perceptible. In his youth the church in Germany was massively present everywhere, not only in a church. There were signs of the faith every place—crosses, shrines, processions, religious habits, Roman collars. One could really *see* the church. This church was the public incarnation and support of one's own personal faith. But now not only the church is questioned but so is Christ. If not dead, God at least seems to be absent. Indeed, is God really necessary or even desirable? Culturally the faith is clearly in need.

What "Bes" It All About?

Now we come to the second dimension of the *Glaubensnot*, the philosophical. "Ontological" is an even better word, since we are now clearly face to face with the question, "What is it all about?" or "What 'bes' it all about?" At times I shall avoid the normal inflections of the verb "to be" and simply use "be." Otherwise we can easily hide from the question of Be-ing behind the grammatical verb forms. Shakespeare put the question most pointedly when he had Hamlet muse, "To be or not to be—that is the question!" Notice, not *a* question, but THE question.

This is the question philosophers and theologians have been asking from the very beginning. Not only these experts, however, but every human being asks this question. We all want to know whether life is worth living. The word BEing makes this inquiry all embracing. It applies the question not only to living beings, but to all being.

German can do so much with one word. Contemporary philosophers often refer to the human being as the *Seinsfrage*, "Being's question." This means two things. In the *human* being, being itself becomes a question. Second, human being, by virtue of its very being, *is* (a) question. This merely puts into words our daily experience. We experience that we really do be, but we also experience that to be is not exhausted in our own being. There are other beings. Furthermore, we ourselves do not always be in the same manner. We change, we grow, we decline, and our being is not always the same in every respect. So we can say that we both be and not be at the same time, although not in the same way. These differences in being cause our human being itself to be a question and they also cause being in general to become a question. Since being "bes" in so many different ways, it is not immediately clear what all these different ways can have in common. If they don't have enough in common, then we are condemned to chaos and nothing at all makes sense, including human being. There is no meaning, for us or anything else. This would be an extreme position, but it is not all that rare among philosophers. It is this question of the meaning of being that all philosophies, theologies, and religions must ask.

Here our focus is on the human being as question. For two reasons I think it is necessary to speak at least briefly of being in general as a question. First of all, Rahner himself insists that even an anthropocentric or anthropological theology must also be ontological or metaphysical. Second, it does not seem possible that we human beings can avoid the ontological question. We ask it essentially and inevitably, even when we are not aware that we are doing it. Unfortunately we must concede that often enough metaphysics does have a bad name, partly because it has too often been associated with a particular school or system of philosophy. In itself metaphysics is as desirable as it is unavoidable. Rahner does not shy away from identifying "metaphysics" with "that absolute longing of the human being," whereby he is superior to both beast and computer (XIV, 15). As a systematic intellectual inquiry, ontology is the unfolding of this "absolute longing" present in our various human experiences. Philosophy or religion is the search for an answer that would satisfy it. Humanity without metaphysics would be a runt.

How does metaphysics actually work? We return to our understanding of the human being as one who not only asks questions, but is (a) question. As Be-ings we question experience (1) that we be; (2) that we also not be; (3) that there is being beyond our own particular being. Furthermore, in our own lives we experience that we surpass our own limited being at any given moment. Although we experience our limits, we also experience that we go beyond these limits. Since we transcend them, we can avoid explictly asking what lies beyond any given limit. However, there seems to be at least one limit which we cannot transcend—the limit of death. Death does not allow us to avoid asking about the nature of this ultimate beyond. Experience of both our limits and our transcendence of these limits compels us to ask the question, "What's it all about?" Or, in the catechism many of us learned: "Where did I come from? Why am I here? Where am I going?" Because we cannot avoid asking these questions, we are all philosophers and theologians.

> For in theology there must be strict thinking. Thinking which questions its very self as a whole and thinks totally is metaphysics. Hence, it is futile to speak of the end of metaphysics. As long as philosophy and theology keep themselves open to questioning . . . they will be able to discover a *philosophia perennis*

in the many different metaphysics which currently exist (VIII,185).

This is but a more complicated way of saying that all human beings ask the question, "What's it all about?" Some of us are professional, most of us "everyday" philosophers. As the latter we are generally "implicit" philosophers. We spontaneously find sufficient reasons for living—in spite of our limits, even that ultimate limit of death. However, at times this general, implicit philosophizing becomes explicit and deliberate and achieves a certain historical visibility. That is, we reflect on our experience and make our reasons for living present to ourselves. We develop definite ideas and concepts to explain what has happened, to make some sense out of it. We can see this most easily in regard to death, and especially the unexpected death of a young person makes us spontaneously ask, "*Why?*"

We try to answer this question by relating the particular event of death to the greater world around us, but even this is not enough. Death forces us to relate our limited being to the unlimited being beyond us. At least in comparison to our limited being it seems unlimited. From the earliest days of Greek philosophy this beyond has been called the *apeiron*, the unlimited or boundless. It has also come to designate the infinite. Although philosophers have placed various values on this apeiron, none has been able to neglect it. *The* question that has dominated all human thinking is the nature of this apeiron. Is it nothing? Is it just more of the same—an eternal cycle? If neither of these, is it better or worse than what we have/be now? A frequent answer to this question is that the apeiron is God. A classic example of this approach is Thomas Aquinas' five ways of showing that God exists. Each proof proceeds from our human experience of limited being to something beyond this limited human being, something "Which all call, name, say to be God" (S.T., q.I, a.2, ad.3).

For Christians this apeiron is not only a beyond that is distant and separated from our world, but is also near and present to us and even in us. This gracious nearness of the apeiron which is also beyond us is most fully present in our history in Jesus. He is revealed by God and discovered by us to be the absolute bringer of salvation. This means that he is the absolute answer to that question of/about being which we are.

It is most fitting then, that pop culture should ask the question "What's it all about?"—not only in general, as the movie *Alfie*, but also directly about Jesus, as Mary Magdalene does in *Jesus Christ Superstar*. Christians claim that Jesus is the answer to this question. "For of all the names in the world . . . this is the only one by which we can be saved" (Acts 4:12). Jesus himself insisted "I am the Way, the Truth and the Life" (John 14:6). It is the conviction of Christians that Jesus both evokes the question in a special way and also provides the answer.

Method

Rahner's entire theological enterprise is concerned with showing that Jesus can be and is the answer to the question which we are. As we know from our own everyday experience, there must be a correspondence between a possible question and a possible answer. This means that if Jesus is the answer to the question which we are, we must be that question in a way which allows and requires Jesus to be the answer. To demonstrate this, Rahner has chosen the transcendental or transcendental-anthropological method, which originated in philosophy. Rahner's transcendental theological method is not the mere imposition of this philosophical method on the Christian faith from the outside. His method is really his own, as he himself indicates:

> If one examines it (my theology) exactly, one finds that it is not so precisely "transcendental-philosophical." It is, rather, the application of the method which was recommended by Vatican I. According to this method, the meaning of a dogma can be really discovered only if one constantly and thoroughly confronts it with (other) faith statements. That is, one must proceed by means of the "analogia fidei" (analogy of faith) more than with the "analogia entis" (analogy of being). There is a further advantage to this procedure. Precisely in this manner both the reasonableness and, if one wishes, the relativity of the dogma are also revealed.[2]

It is important to note that Rahner says not "instead of" but "more than." He also adds explictly that even in the "analogy of faith" at least a "little bit of logic" is not only indispensable but also desirable.

In Rahner's theologizing, for himself and for others, the starting point is always the already graced human being. Rahner's method presupposes precisely someone who already believes, for whatever reason, and who wonders whether he or she can still believe in an intellectually honest manner. Theology has always been concerned with this question. Of late its answer has been divided into three branches: fundamental, dogmatic-systematic, and ascetical-mystical theology. The fundamental proves that Christian, supernatural revelation is not intrinsically contradictory and therefore not impossible. It goes on to show that such a revelation has happened in the Judeo-Christian religious tradition, which culminates in Jesus Christ. To his life, death, and resurrection there are trustworthy historical data and witnesses. This witness is handed on, in and by the church. Systematic-dogmatic theology proves and develops the value of Jesus and his concern (*die Sache Jesu*) for the world. Ascetical-mystical theology explains how human being, constituted in this Jesus, is to be lived personally and socially. How human consciousness, already expanded on earth by grace, moves toward its culmination in the beatific vision of God in heaven is the matter of this third branch of theology.

Rahner has often reproached both this division of theology and the actual performance of theology for what he calls "extrinsecism." He claims that there is not sufficient integration of the "that" and the "what" of the Christian message. He is especially critical of the gap between fundamental theology's proof of the "fact" of Christian revelation and dogmatic-systematic's explanation of the "content." This problem has been made more severe by the Enlightenment's insistence on an explicit explanation of how the "accidental" (the contingent) can be necessary and thus "obligatory." For Christians the challenge here is clear. How can a historical person like Jesus be of critical, indeed absolute importance? This challenge is further complicated by the competing and conflicting pluralism of philosophies and cultures in our modern world.

In order to respond to precisely this condition of the ontological and cultural *Glaubensnot* of contemporary human beings, Rahner has had recourse to the transcendental method. The extrinsecism of past theology can be overcome and the challenge of contemporary pluralism met. The transcendental method does not concentrate its reflection on the individual contents/ of systematic theology but on believing human Christians themselves. It analyzes the constitution of the human being to see how the act of faith is possible at all and *act*-ual in any given case. Again, unlike the extrinsecist theology he reproaches, Rahner does not pretend that he is an unbeliever. He does not act as if Jesus has not lived and then try to prove the claims of Christianity. He does not act like an outsider or a presumably unbiased, objective observer. Here, as always, Rahner assumes both explicit, categorical, historical Christianity and the transcendental experience of the already graced human being. He says explictly of himself and his theologizing:

> I always want to make the human being aware that, whether he is reflectively aware of it or not, whether he accepts or represses it or not, he does have an experience of grace from within. This is the most original and most important root of all Christian piety and holiness.[3]

Of course, this experience of grace must also have an objective, categorical expression in history and society. The most intimate personal experiences are never only and purely interior. They are always experienced within the framework of interpretations or doctrines provided by the pre-existing society or tradition, whether civil or ecclesial.

Rahner insists that

> the preacher of the Gospel never encounters an atheist who has had simply no experience of God whatsoever ... as if the existence of God were to be proved like that of an object which is accessible through merely *a posteriori* experience, and which ... could be justly rejected without hesitation as being of no interest to begin with, and certainly not worth the effort which would be required to investigate it.
>
> What is important is to help the human being understand that there is an entirely different kind of experience, namely a transcendental one. In this experience of spiritual knowing and freedom we are able to know what we call God. We can be and are conscious of his reality. This transcendental experience points to God. It is also the condition which makes any and all *a posteriori* experience possible, in life in general and

in knowing in particular. This transcendental experience is present and operative in all *a posteriori* experience. This remains true even though this everyday experience is not able to reflect on and explicate its own proper presuppositions (VIII, 204-206).

This lengthy citation is fitting because it shows how Rahner himself justifies his choice of the transcendental method. It is not precisely a matter of philosophy but of theology. For Rahner theology itself is precisely an initiation or "mystagogy into the absolute mystery which [already] pervades our very existence and being" (VIII, 207). Theology is not merely or even primarily academic indoctrination and cannot be. Because of the "supernatural existential," which we shall discuss shortly, theology is always meditation on the revealed truth already present in the Christian. Like everything else in Karl Rahner's theology, the transcendental method also stands completely in the service of the universal saving will of God. We can now elaborate Rahner's own understanding and use of the transcendental method. Then we shall see how God's universal saving will takes the form of the supernatural existential in Rahner's theology.

Transcendental Method

Why did Rahner choose the transcendental method? Not because it is the only legitimate method of theologizing, although it does enjoy a certain preferred status in Western thought, especially since Kant. However, it has been present in certain ways throughout all of Western philosophy, in Plato, Aristotle, Augustine, Aquinas, certainly Descartes. In theology the analysis of the act of faith was intended to show how the absolute assent of faith to the word of God was possible at all. In one sense the transcendental method is not all that new. However, the term and approach have received a definite character and identity from Kant. His description has become normative: the investigation into the conditions presupposed by or necessary for any knowledge. Nevertheless, the concepts to which Kant gave "definite" form were soon modified. Rahner agrees that his theology can be called "transcendental" because it has a certain affinity with and parentage from Kant's philosophy.

However, as we have already seen, Rahner does not simply repeat Kant, nor does he insist on the name "transcendental."

For Rahner transcendental philosophy or theology is not a set body of doctrines and ideas. It is a particular way of asking the question of being and is performed on the human being. As we have seen, human being is such that it can question and must be questioned. On this human "object" Rahner reflects transcendentally. In an interview Rahner was obviously delighted when he caught the interviewer himself referring to Rahner's transcendental theology as a "method."[4] Clearly, Rahner's "debt" to Kant is neither the latter's content nor his presuppositions.[5]

"If reflection on the conditions of concrete existence is called transcendental, then I would call what I do in theology transcendental" (Simons, 36). Admittedly, the origin of transcendental philosophy in Kant was precisely with the philosophical problem of knowing. It is also true that Rahner's own association with the transcendental approach was initially philosophical, precisely in regard to the problem of human knowledge. However, Rahner has repeatedly insisted that his doctoral dissertation is concerned with the metaphysics of human knowing, not with epistemology or the critique of knowing as such. His examination of an article in St. Thomas Aquinas' *Summa Theologiae* (I, q.84, a.7) confronts Aquinas' assertion of the necessity of the intellect's conversion to the phantasm in human knowing with questions from Kant, Heidegger, and Hegel. Immediately after this "purely speculative" philosophical work, Rahner moved on to the philosophy of religion.

In *Hearers of the Word* he reflects transcendentally on revelation. He examines the ability of the human being to hear a possibly divine revelation, not as a supposedly disinterested objective outsider, but precisely as a believing Christian. Concretely, Rahner uses the transcendental method of reflection to show how free, knowing human beings are able to receive precisely that revelation which Christianity claims to have been given. The transcendental method does not prove that Christianity can happen, although (as if) it has not yet happened. It does not deduce Christianity's possibility and necessity from some "pure" human nature or from some abstract idea of being. In spite of Rahner's repeated denials, some people claim that this is what transcendental theology does. That is simply not the case! Rahner's transcendental method always presupposes the Christian world and history in which we actually live. He says explicitly: "It is not the case that I could use the transcendental method to develop a Christology unless I already actually believed in Jesus Christ" (Simons, 51). Once Jesus has actually existed, Christians are still faced with a critical question. Can they honestly and humanly believe that Jesus is the Son of God, without, as one of Rahner's best bon mots puts it, "the harakiri of the absurdity of faith"? To answer precisely this question Rahner has found the method of transcendental reflection preferable.

Transcendental reflection on the human being reveals that so-called created human nature is able to receive a higher, greater communication of being from God than it has already received in creation, if God chooses to grant it. Theology has termed this transcendental nature or capacity an "obediential potency." It has the potentiality to receive that greater communication of being which Christian tradition calls supernatural grace and revelation. Why is this possible? Because the very nature of the human being as spirit implies a capacity or dynamism for absolute being. It is important, once again, to note that Rahner's transcendental reflection does not establish this merely as an abstract idea or ideal possibility. In the real world in which we really exist this is the actual state of affairs. His reflection starts not with an idea or a concept, not even with the substance or essence of the human being, but with the experienced real act of the acting human being. Rahner discloses this absolute dynamism by examining the actual performance of the knowing subject and lays bare those conditions which are necessary for the possibility of this act of knowing.

The key word here is *spirit*. It translates the German word *Geist*, which could also be translated *mind*. For various historical reasons which we need not examine, spirit has become the preferred translation. However, the word *spirit* is not without its own difficulties. Too often it is associated with invisible and consequently with unreal. Invisibility is not its most important characteristic. For our purposes emphasis will be placed on spirit as a being which has intellect, will, and freedom. Spirit means that one can know, love, and choose and that one is free. As spirit, one is aware of oneself. One is the self-presence of knowing and loving. One's consciousness does not end with oneself or any particular act of knowing or choosing. It always stretches beyond itself. It is a thrust toward the absolute. It requires and implies a real pre-apprehension of unlimited Being. Again we meet the apeiron. As spirit in the world, that is, an embodied spirit, one is a receptive knower. One's self-knowledge is possible only by virtue of prior affirmation of sensible realities, which are not simply identical with one's mind. One's knowledge is not intuition or innate ideas. It is not the pure identity of God or some substitute from the philosophy of absolute idealism. Like one's being, one's knowledge is also "discursive." It is spread out through time and space. Human being is not simply consciousness but also matter. Hence, human being is not simply the actual identity of being and consciousness in act. One gradually becomes aware of one's own existence as free and knowing in one's knowing of sensible objects. One distinguishes these objects from one's self in the very act of knowing, and places them "against" one's own proper self. This is the experience and consciousness of difference by limitation. It is possible only because the inherent dynamism of the intellect enables it to recognize implicitly but really the "more" of unlimited being. This unlimited being makes both the existence and recognition of limited being possible. Thus, because of what it actually does in any given act of knowing, the human intellect is seen to have an implicit pre-conceptual reaching out toward infinite Being.

This "reaching out" is called unthematic, because it is not an actual theme or explicit idea which reflective thinking has developed. It is not a definite, de-fined idea. It is likewise called a pre-grasp. This word is an attempt to translate the German *Vorgriff*, which is also translated "pre-apprehension." Here it is a matter of distinguishing between what actually happens and the explicit, reflective explanation of what happens. Rahner claims that every limited act of human being is possible only because there is unlimited being. This unlimited being is called the horizon. It not only limits but also, and indeed primarily, makes possible. This horizon is not only unlimited in fact but must be unlimited, for if it were not unlimited, it would be limited itself. Then the original problem would return: How is the limited, the finite, the contingent possible at all? Because this horizon is necessarily unlimited, it is said to be absolute.

Rahner claims that the method of transcendental reflection on human activity shows that the finite and infinite are not in hostile conflict with another, nor are they separated by an infinite abyss. Rather, they are related in such a way that the infinite enables the finite to be. This, in turn, enables the finite to enjoy an inner dynamism for the infinite. Finite being necessarily strives toward, moves, reaches out for the infinite. Perhaps another world where this would not be the case is thinkable. But our experience of the real, actual world in which we live reveals that the apeiron, the unlimited beyond, is positively related to the limited here and now.

We can now recall our understanding of the human being as the question from and about being. The human being can and must question. Even the denial of human nature as question cannot escape its inevitability. This denial is itself questionable. Furthermore, every question, if answered, gives rise to another question. The answer itself is questionable, leading not to regression but to an infinite progression. Question and answer do reveal the limits of human being, but they also simultaneously reveal the unlimitedness of the being beyond human being. As we saw, this beyond cannot itself be limited. That would only postpone, repeat, or camouflage the question and not provide the answer. The beyond cannot be nothing. As Rahner so simply states, "nothingness grounds nothing."[6] Hence, according to Rahner's method of transcendental reflection on human activity, the only source of real, limited being is revealed to be real unlimited being—God, according to Thomas Aquinas.

Through this more philosophical transcendental reflection Rahner has been able to show that Judeo-Christianity's claims about the Beyond and its relationship to this world cannot be dismissed out of hand. They are not inherently absurd or unthinkable. He does *not* show that these claims are thinkable in some purely philosophical exercise. He does not assert that these claims can be deduced from some pure concept of being. He does argue that, given the historical existence cf the Judeo-Christian tradition, its claims deserve a hearing from humanity. It is possible that these claims contain the answer to the question which human beings are and which their own mental reflection has made them aware of being.

Rahner's transcendental theological method "mediates" between the "changeless a priori structure of the human mind, which, as Lonergan has shown, is the unrevisable revisor of all conceptual frameworks,"[7] and the historically contingent revelation of Christ, whom Christianity proclaims as the answer to that infinite questioning which transcendental philosophical reflection has shown the human being to be. Practically, this means that in their daily lives people are not merely meaninglessly tossed to and fro from one isolated individual event to another. Rather, "in these very mundane everyday activities the human being experiences that, occupied with the grains of sand on the beach, he lives on the shore of the infinite mystery" (IX, 170).

To show that this is the case Karl Rahner developed his theory of the supernatural existential. This theory, one of his most controversial, is his attempt to explain how God's universal saving will actually affects the world. It is one of Rahner's most decisive efforts to avoid that extrinsecism which we noted earlier. Consequently, it is a serious effort to present supernatural grace in such a way that humans cannot be indifferent to it, and is also a good example of how Rahner philosophizes in theology. In this instance it is the philosophy of Heidegger which provides the starting point.

Supernatural Existential

We should recall Rahner's years with Heidegger from whom comes the term "existential." The most discernible influence of Heidegger on Rahner is to be found in his manner of asking questions, the manner of philosophizing. Heidegger developed the term "existential" to explicate merely natural finite human being and existence. Rahner uses it, on the other hand, to explicate the precisely supernatural existence of human being in the actual world of God's universal saving will. William Richardson, the "American Heidegger" as Rahner once described him, gives this description of existential, which should serve as an admonition to those who complain about Rahner's language and style:

Since existence for Heidegger is that structure by which There-being [=*Dasein*=the Human Being], thrown among beings, comprehends their Being, only that is existential which pertains to There-being's comprehension of the Being-structure of beings, hence to the primordial constitution of There-being itself. The term pertains to existence in its ontological dimension.[8]

In Heidegger's vocabulary, existential is contrasted to *existentiell*. This latter term corresponds to what we have called that everyday cultural dimension of our *Glaubensnot*. Existential corresponds to what we have called the ontological dimension. In both cases there is distinction between the two terms, but not separation. They are two dimensions of the same reality, finite human being. These are common "categories" in Rahner's thought and vocabulary.

When Rahner speaks of the supernatural existential, he wants to describe how the human being actually exists in the real world. The ontological constitution and status of human being in this world is supernatural, because it is in fact constituted in grace by the universal saving will of God. Since the human is graced, one of the human's existentials is supernatural. Unfortunately, this term was immediately caught up in the customary scholastic controversies about nature and grace, natural and supernatural, the natural desire to see God and the gratuity of grace. The reaction to this theory has been complicated by a misunderstanding of his use of the transcendental method. Consequently Rahner has often been accused of limiting God's power, of reducing the supernatural to the natural, of voiding grace of its gratuity.

No one who has seriously studied Rahner could so accuse him. As we have seen, neither by nature nor by philosophy nor by transcendental philosophical analysis is the human being prepared for grace. Neither is this human being thus enabled to require, demand, or earn it. Rather, in the real graced world the transcendental method reveals or uncovers the conditions, both transcendental and historical, which are required for what has come to be termed theologically revelation, grace, glory.

The transcendental nature of the human being is seen to be an obediential potency for whatever further sharing may please God. From the concrete historical experience and tradition of the Judeo-

Christian revelation we know that God wills the salvation of all. Consequently, transcendent human nature is obedientially potent in a graced world. The human being actually experiences and transcends limits in a world in which God has established Himself as the personal apeiron and proper end of human transcending. Thus, in the real world, human transcendence in act has as its "natural" outcome intimate personal communion with God. Supernatural existential means that God has provided the world with an ontological horizon other than some other possible world might have had. Since this horizon is God, it is called grace. In the really existing world there is a "natural" desire for the beatific vision (1 Corinthians 13:12), but not because of some presumed ability of the human being as such. Not human being, but precisely the divine being is the cause of this desire. The being of the world and of the human being therein are the graced world of the universally saving God. This graced world is a real-ontological determination of the human being. It precedes and thus constitutes the conditions of the existence of individual human beings. Therefore it is said to condition existentially their action, cognition, and volition. This is the meaning of the supernatural existential.

It does not destroy the gratuity of grace. It does powerfully remind us that there has never ever been a merely, purely human nature. Human beings have never really existed without an ontological, existential, *existentiell* relationship to Christian grace and salvation. Consequently "pure nature" is a remainder concept (*Restbegriff*). Even better, pure nature is purely a theological construct. It enables us to better contemplate the incomprehensible riches of the God who has given his very self as gift to the non-godly (Romans 11:33-36). Pure nature is a theological theory. It means that an intelligent, free human nature other than the one God actually created, whose finality is the beatific vision, is not a priori and intrinsically unthinkable. This remains true no matter how unsuccessful all efforts at a precise explication of this other, unreal human nature have been. Here one need only recall the dead ends of theological speculation about the possible natural end of a merely natural human being.

The problem of nature and grace, especially the gratuity of grace, has preoccupied theologians ever since Baius (1513-89) tried to root grace as deeply as possible in human nature. Contemporary and subsequent counterattacks on Baius intended to preserve the gratuity of grace. However, they also tended to make this necessary but certainly secondary characteristic of grace the dominant concern of theology about grace.[9] The result of Baius' effort was just the opposite of what he desired: The gap between the natural and supernatural was not contracted but expanded. Grace had become even more extrinsic to human nature, both ontologically and historically.

A major consequence of this anti-Baian approach was support for a theological opinion which eventually enjoyed almost universal acceptance: In the real order there are human acts which are truly but merely good (*actus naturaliter honesti*). They are without grace as their source or salvation as their end. This opinion certainly divides the one creation of God into two worlds. One is natural and contributes nothing to salvation. The other is supernatural and separate from everyday life, at least in principle. Against this clearly extrinsecist understanding of nature and grace Rahner's supernatural existential is directed. The same applies to the voluntarist and nominalist misconception that the human being's orientation to a supernatural end is constituted merely by an external divine decree. The supernatural existential asserts that, in the world to which God has actually given existence, grace is an existential of human being. It is an inner ontological constituent of the world. Grace is not merely actual, but also habitual, not merely created, but also uncreated. Therefore grace does not merely elevate individual and disparate human acts. It elevates the very being of human nature. All precisely human actions—knowing, choosing, loving—happen within a horizon that is supernatural. In Thomistic terms, their formal object is the gracing and saving God. They have their own proper and peculiar perfection. They are not merely "natural" acts to which a supernatural dignity is decreed from without. They are, rather, the supernatural acts of a graced, elevated consciousness. This remains true even though they happen to look just like merely natural human acts. The "experience of grace in everyday life" has been present in Rahner's thought from the very beginning, especially in his devotional and mystical writings. Now it may very well be the dominant theme of his writings. To prevent a dualism between the grace that has been poured out into our hearts (Romans 5:2-5) and our daily lives is the purpose of Rahner's theology of the supernatural existential. Indeed, it is the purpose of his entire theology. For this reason he has used the method of transcendental reflection. His purpose has been neither to force God to grace humans nor to limit his actual gracing. It has been to show that God created the human being precisely so that he or she can be graced. It is in this context that the lapidary statement of *Hearers of the Word* is to be understood. "God can reveal only that which the human being can hear. This sentence is immediately clearly intelligible." This does not mean, of course, that the human being determines the divine being. In the same book Rahner insists: "This revelation of God cannot be grounded and justified in human being—not in its factualness, not in its necessity, not in its inner essence."[10]

Rahner rejects extrinsecism, which would reduce Christianity to mythology. He also rejects a certain type of intrinsecism which would reduce Christianity to modernism, in which case it would be merely one more humanism among many other equally valid ones. There is a traditional term in theology which best describes Rahner's approach to God and humanity, grace, and nature. It is "perichoresis" and comes from Christology and the theology of the Trinity. The word itself is composed of two Greek words which mean "to dance around with." It was used to describe the relationship between the divine and human in Jesus as well as the relationships among Father, Son, and Holy Spirit in the Trinity. In both cases the relationship is that of being pleased with the other. Perichoresis describes an intensely intimate communion which does not suppress the members, but allows them to thrive and flourish. This most aptly describes the relationship of the divine and human in Rahner's theology. This perichoresis is perfectly present in Jesus Christ, as we shall shortly see, and is also present, as much as it can be, in all human beings because they live in a world which has been graced by God.

Christology

For Rahner there is no antinomy among theocentric, Christocentric, and anthropocentric theologies. He rejects explicitly the accusation of having reduced the Christian to the (merely) human. He has not sneakily transformed a theocentric anthropology into an anthropocentric theology:

I would say this simply and with great conviction: if one does anthropology correctly and from the very beginning observes those limitations which it has of its very own and which need not be imposed from outside, then, such an anthropology can in no wise be in opposition to a theocentric theology. Why? Not only because in his very origin and being man [has] simple and radical openness to God as the absolute mystery, but also because the dynamism of the self-communication of God (known as Grace, Holy Spirit) is also equally at work from the very beginning. Thus, as soon as we live this inner gracedness historically, we are already in the realm of revelation. To objectify this lived grace in history by putting it into concepts and words is to do theology, indeed, a theocentric theology.[11]

A clear consequence of this is that there must be Christology from above and below. At least in theory they are complementary and cannot be contradictory. Obviously, all Christology is originally from below, for there could be no Christology at all without there first having been a Christ in history. This repetition is warranted because Rahner is continually accused of being a cryptic absolute idealist who can transcendentally deduce the idea of Christ and Christianity from some pure idea of being. In the above interview he compares music and Christology: "I only know what music is when I have experienced Bach and Beethoven and Mozart. Afterwards, on the basis of such a concrete historical encounter I can ask philosophical and metaphysical questions. . . . I must also be able to show that the concrete history which is named Jesus has an inner relatedness to the original, primary—and, if you will, transcendental—constitution of the human being" (p. 141). Again, it is a matter of perichoresis between the ontological and the cultural-historical. If Jesus is of "only" historical interest to me, could he be of absolute importance to me? But Christianity has claimed that Jesus is of absolute importance to all human beings (Acts 4:12). In Jesus there must be perichoresis between his ontological person and his historical mission. Likewise, between the person of Jesus and human onotology and human history there must also be perichoresis. To establish this perichoresis theologically is the special task of Christology.

Rahner acknowledges that in recent years his Christology has concentrated less on what he calls "descent Christology" and more on "ascent Christology." These approaches to the theology of Christ are also called descending and ascending as well as Christologies from above and below. The former start with the eternal God and proceed to the historical Jesus; the latter start with the historical Jesus and proceed to the eternal God. This is not because the approach emphasizing that God became human and world history is wrong. However, it is true that this metaphysical approach, which starts with the transcendent God, was more at home in an earlier thought world. While this more speculative approach need not be abandoned, it is not the only legitimate one. One can begin just as well with the living, dead, and resurrected Jesus. Wherever one starts, one must always face the problem of history and transcendence. Neither starting point guarantees a satisfactory solution to this problem, for each has its own intrinsic temptation. Christology from above will be tempted to shortshrift the historical, Christology from below the transcendent. In this context Rahner emphasizes that even in his earliest writings he was concerned to show that human transcendence is and happens historically. He had already laid the foundations for later developments in his Christology.

Christology can serve as the nexus of theology and anthropology. If Christ is who the Christian tradition asserts him to be, Christology prods us to examine our understanding of both God and humans. Both must be in themselves in such a way that they can be together in Christ. The traditional assertion that in Jesus there is a hypostatic union of two natures in one person retains permanent validity. However, this technical formulation is not the only possible one, nor is it to be regarded as simply intelligible and preachable. In fact, it may remain unintelligible even to those of good will and good mind. Hence, other ways of explaining and expressing the union of the divine and the human in Jesus must be sought.

The philosophical and general cultural pluralism of our contemporary world both requires and enables other explanations. This pluralism requires great mutual tolerance on the part of the ecclesiastical magisterium, theological specialists, and the faithful at large. The great variety of contemporary philosophies as well as the knowledge explosion in general and in theology in particular render the evaluation of conceptual, verbal, doctrinal orthodoxy increasingly difficult.

Hence, in both securing and discerning doctrinal and confessional orthodoxy, liturgical worship will play a much more important role. For
example, in the Roman Catholic Church continued celebration of the
Eucharist may be a much more reliable indicator of the orthodoxy of
a theologian's faith than one's verbal statements in explanation of
that faith.

A discussion of pluralism is important here for two reasons. First
of all, theologians who try to develop a contemporary Christology in
and for the new pluralism are very likely to come under suspicion.
The protectors of orthodoxy in their various churches are more likely
to be upset by new Christological theories than other ones. Hence, a
proper understanding of the new pluralism is crucial for the protec-
tion of theologians. Second, I think that it illustrates the fundamental
principle of all Rahner's transcendental theology. His transcendental
reflection, analysis, and deduction always begins with the "facts."
Were there no pluralism in fact, Rahner would not attempt to theolo-
gize it. Likewise, had there been no Jesus in history, whose memory is
present to us in the tradition, Rahner would not attempt transcendental Christology. The transcendental deduction of the idea of Christ is
entirely dependent on the historical Jesus. Rahner also never tires of
repeating that, once history has happened, there is no one absolutely
exclusive way of explaining it, however privileged any given way may
be in any given time and place. Rahner fully accepts the relativity of
his own Christology. For Rahner, Christology is essentially soteriolo-
gy. That is, as Jesus is essentially savior, so is Christology essentially
the study of the savior of the human race. The passage of Jesus—his
death, resurrection, glorification—reveals him to have been the absolute bringer of salvation. Other "saviors" are neither eliminated nor
denigrated, but are accorded their own particular value in the history
of the becoming flesh of God's creative and salvific will. It is often
asserted that "the blatant consequence of Rahner's Christology is his
proclamation of anonymous Christianity."[12] But one can equally assert that Rahner's explicit Christology is the consequence of what can
be called his "anonymously Christian ontology of creatureliness."[13]
Jesus is neither a mythological freak nor so singular that he must remain in splendid isolation. Isolation is precisely what Jesus is not, for
Jesus is most properly the communion of the Godly with the not-

godly. Creation without incarnation is not unthinkable. But at best it would be a deficient mode of that of which God is capable. When God becomes the not-godly, Christ is what preeminently happens. Cosmic and human being are the contextual concomitant of the Christ. "Thus, we may quite calmly say that what we call creation is a partial moment (*Teilmoment*) of God's Becoming-world (*Weltwerdung*). God factually and freely utters himself in his Logos who has become world and matter" (V, 205).

Some of Rahner's most difficult pages are, as one might expect, his musings on John 1:14. He has been accused of Hegelianism because he has concluded that God truly can *become* in the other. Rahner's concern is neither Hegelian nor some sort of pure philosophizing. Here, as elsewhere, Rahner's concern is entirely theological—to further understand the congeniality of the divine and human which was revealed absolutely in Jesus. This congeniality in Jesus is described by the term "hypostatic union." In Jesus are present both God's absolute self-communication to and affirmation of humanity and humanity's absolute acceptance and transcendence into God. Henceforth, God's self-communication to the not-godly is utterly irrevocable, not only in the divine will but also in human history. Consequently, if death means not being at all anymore, Jesus *had* to be raised from the dead. Otherwise God's self-communication would have been undone. In context this would also mean that God himself had been undone. He would have been revealed to be the weaker, not the stronger (Luke 11:21). The kingdom of death would have been revealed to be stronger than the kingdom of life (Matthew 16:16-19).

Thus Jesus is the unique and absolute bringer of salvation. The uniqueness of Jesus is for us, not against us. The hypostatic union is not primarily the special privilege of Jesus as an individual but is, rather,

> an inner moment of the total gracing of spiritual creatures in general. In Christ God's self-communication happens fundamentally for all. It happens in humanity. Insofar as this unsurpassable self-communication of God "is there" in an historically irrevocable and graspable mode and insofar as it is conscious of itself, we can speak of hypostatic union. Thus the hypostatic union does not differ from our grace by what is pledged in it if one may so speak. In both cases this is grace

(also in Jesus). The difference is that Jesus is the pledge of this grace for us. But we are not, in our turn, further pledges, but the recipients of God's pledge to us (V, 210-212).

As mediator of God's universal saving will, Jesus does not come between us and God as a medium by which we would still be apart. Rather Jesus the mediator comes between us precisely as the medium in which we are one. "The mediation of the man Jesus to God does not undo immediacy to God, but precisely constitutes it" (VIII, 234).

Trinity

Ultimately this self-communication of God to the not-godly in nature, grace, and glory is possible only because God is who he is. God is originally and fundamentally triune. In his writings on the Trinity Rahner has striven diligently to avoid that implicitly heretical theology which starts with one God and subsequently divides this one divine nature into three persons. The one God is one precisely because and insofar as he is "three-personed." "The doctrine of the Trinity cannot and must not be understood as either a supplement or a debilitation of Christian monotheism. It is, rather, its radicalization. The only presupposition is that this monotheism is taken seriously as the concrete monotheism of salvation history's experience. This concrete monotheism does not remove from God his unicity (*Einzigkeit*), as Christian salvation history has experienced him, and exile him into an abstract metaphysical, lonely aloneness (*Einsamkeit*)" (XIII, 133).

Too often in academic theology as well as popular piety and catechesis God's being is divided into three people. The original unity in diversity and diversity in unity which the true doctrine of the Trinity contains and which God needs to be pure act and infinite being is then lost. Attempts to remedy this implicit tritheism often end in a monism which masquerades as monotheism.

Rahner suggests that in future trinitarian theology the term *person* will play a steadily decreasing role. Here we also have a good example of Rahner's dedication to the tradition of theology and church. Increasingly uneasy with the suitability of the term *person*, he does not feel empowered to dispense with it on his own. Why? "The magisterium forbids [the theologian] to suppress such concepts on his own authority, but also obliges him to work at their fuller explanation. This he can do only if he uses other words for the official ecclesiastical concepts which are to be explained" (XII, 133).

Trinitarian theology also affords us another occasion to consider Rahner's theological method. Rahner does not discover the Trinity through introspective self-contemplation and consequent transcendental deduction from his own subjectivity. He starts with the "facts" of Judeo-Christian history and revelation. On this basis he develops his theory of God as triune. It emphasizes that the inner life of God is expressed positively in his action outwardly in the world. Thus the immanent Trinity (God in himself) is understood to be the economic Trinity of salvation history (God in the world).

Salvation history reveals and enables us to understand that God's very being is communion, communication, sharing. However, this sharing does not and could not just happen in general. Then it would not really be communion. The experience of Jesus reveals a triple relationship within the triune being. The Christian tradition has been able to discern this relationship as Father, Son, and Holy Spirit. That this inner specificity should be preserved in the theology of God's creating and saving relationship with the world has been one of Rahner's emphases. He has urged that the pre-Augustinian and Eastern understanding of the Trinity be reactivated in Western theology. The monist threat inherent in the Augustinian psychological approach could be contained by this more balanced theology. Furthermore, the piety of the Christian people would also be enriched:

> Nowadays when we speak of God's incarnation, the theological and religious emphasis lies only on the fact that "God" became man, that "one" of the divine persons (of the Trinity) took on the flesh, and not on the fact that this person is precisely the person of the Logos. One has the feeling that, for the catechism of head and heart (as contrasted with the printed catechism), the Christian's idea of the incarnation would not have to change at all if there were no Trinity. For God would still, as (the one) person, have become man, which is in fact about all the average Christian explicitly grasps when he confesses the incarnation. There must surely be more than one voluminous modern scientific Christology which never makes it very clear exactly *which* divine hypostasis has assumed human nature.[14]

Symbol

The trinitarian parentage of Rahner's theory of the symbol is obvious. First of all, the real ontological symbol must be distinguished from the merely conventional, utilitarian, informational sign. Symbol does have something in common with such arbitrary signs—both make known more than immediately meets the eye. However, the difference is crucial. There is an organic ontological unity between the symbol and that of which it is the symbol. The symbol is the appearance, the manifestation, the phenomenon of another being. In other words, there is symbol when a real being expresses itself in another by making itself present in this other being. Non-identity is necessary for symbol. Equally necessary is a connatural unity between that which is symbolized and the symbol itself. In the Trinity, for example, the Father is precisely Father insofar as he utters himself in the Logos, who is distinct from but in union with him. This Logos or Word is the image of the Father. Another example is the Thomistic doctrine of the soul as the substantial form of the body. The soul exists insofar as it embodies and thus expresses itself in the body. In turn, the body is distinct from the soul, but not a separate part. The body is the phenomenon, the mode of the soul's presence and appearance. Likewise, historical persons become who they are in the act of expressing and in the expression of themselves. A gesture is not merely an empty, meaningless ritual, which could just as well be present or not. The gesture is the symbol in which the gesturing person becomes that which has been symbolized in the gesture. Through such gestures or symbols the persons actually become themselves. They achieve or create their own precise self and identity. Easy examples of such gesture-symbols are the kiss and the handshake.

The theology of the real-ontological symbol is present and efficacious throughout all of Rahner's thought. The Logos is the eternal symbol of the Father-God. Jesus is the historical symbol of the Logos. The church as tradition is the spatio-temporal symbol of the Christ-Jesus. The seven sacraments, the sacred Scriptures, the sinful yet holy members of the church are the symbols of the church. In each instance it is not a matter of the latter member forcing the former to be or act in a certain way. Rather, it is always the latter which has received its being and identity from the former.

The Motive of the Incarnation: Theiosis

It is consequent that, through the Logos, God's eternal other, the world, should be created. From this point-of-view it is also "natural" for God to create, although it is supernatural from the world's point-of-view to be created. This statement in no way places in God a necessity to create. It merely seeks in God the necessary condition of the possibility of creation. It finds this in the symbolic nature of the triune divine being. All the realities of salvation history—hypostatic union, grace, beatific vision, church, sacraments—can be traced back to the same condition of their possibility. The triune communion nature of God does not make creation and historical salvation necessary. It does make them possible and fitting. We discover this salvation as well as its conditions only after it has become reality.

Sin and death are the two forces which threaten the annihilation of the fragile and failing human being. In Rahner's theology they are immediately and ultimately relativized. God's relationship to the non-godly is originally maximalist. Rahner sides with the Scotists against the Thomists in the dispute about the precise motive of the incarnation. For the Thomistic school of theology the Word would not have become flesh had Adam not sinned. For the Scotist school the Word would have become flesh even if Adam had not sinned. There are texts in the Bible as well as the creeds and councils which both sides invoke to support their positions. The conflict is at least partly rooted in an excessive preoccupation with sin and with a consequently narrow understanding of salvation as chiefly redemption from sin. For Rahner, God initially intended the hypostatic union. Jesus is originally an ontological savior, for he enables finite being to *be*. We can say that in Jesus creation is saved from not being. In the context of a sinful creation Jesus also becomes a hamartiological savior, for he is the friend and forgiver of sinners. In Jesus human weakness, whether ontological or hamartiological, has been assumed by God and within this assumption transformed into strength. In this matter Rahner is much more like the Eastern theologians who emphasize *theiosis* than the Western theologians who emphasize redemption from sin.

Theiosis is a Greek word which can be translated as "divinization." It stresses that the relationship between God and humanity is essentially one in which the human becomes divine. Its classical statement is that God became human in order that humans might become God. In this view the organic, dynamic unity of creation, incarnation, and enspiriting is strikingly clear. The influence and presence of this Eastern emphasis in Rahner's theology is clear and has been rightly noted. It is also clearly congenial to Rahner's philosophical approach to theology Theiosis is not the self-achievement of the creature as distinct or separate from God. It is possible precisely because the creature's being is relatedness to God. This relatedness is the naturally unlimited transcendence of human being. By grace it has been further elevated to immediacy with God himself. Henceforth its only possible end is eternal life with God in the face-to-face encounter we call heaven. According to both Rahner and theiosis theology, this divinizing conversation between God and humankind has truly begun already on earth.

> The proper understanding of grace reveals that it has three dimensions. Philosophically it is possibility. Theologically it is actual reality. *Existentiell* it is realized in hope, thematically or unthematically. According to this understanding, the experience of transcendence that is the experience of God, is also always the experience of grace in the world which really and actually exists. This is the case because the experience of transcendence is radically and dynamically borne by the self-communication of God which makes all this possible and which is located at the very center of our existence. We call this divine self-communication grace and the Holy Spirit. It is both the goal and the power which enables the human being to move toward this goal. It is present in all human beings, at least as a grace offered to their free decision (XIII, 236).

A consequence of Rahner's emphasis on the universal saving will of God and the theory of the supernatural existential is a certain optimism about salvation (*Heilsoptimismus*). This optimism is not supercilious. A certain heaviness bordering on melancholy is discernible in him and his theology. Not restricted to the "hunger years" at the end of World War II when it would certainly have been understandable, this attitude persists even now when Germany has become the *Wirtschaftswunderland* (the land of the economic miracle). Nor is it to be explained solely as that middle European *Weltschmerz* (cosmic pain) which traditionally afflicts German intellectuals. The roots are deeper, and they are ontological. During the earthly life of the historical creature simple identity of consciousness and being is not attainable. Neither is one able to be absolutely certain that the fundamental option of his personal life is in fact for God. It could be against God and hence against being. It cannot be denied—the non-being always lurks on the shadowy side of human existence. Heidegger described the human being as *Sein zum Tode* (being toward and for the sake of death). Rahner did not learn this only from his old teacher. His own experience, one in which we all share as finite creatures, is by far the best teacher in this matter.

Death

The method of transcendental reflection is applied not only to the whole Christian tradition but also to the individual Christian's life. Consequently death, the ultimate threat to being and the inescapable one, has often been a topic of Rahner's consideration. In death the human being is brought face-to-face with the apeiron, the beyond. Is death really the one limit beyond which only not-being or nothing "is"? The very words of the question hint the answer. Rahner's transcendental analysis of the human acts of knowing and choosing reveals that such limited acts are possible only because being as such is unlimited. Hence, death is not simply the beginning of nothing. Since science "does not really know why all multicellular life, and especially man, dies,"[15] an adequate understanding of dying and death cannot be merely biological. It must also be philosophical and theological. Death is that external event which summons the historical and thus processual human being to take stock of his personal becoming. This personal history is constituted by many individual human acts. The crucial question called forth by death is this: is this personal history a becoming that surpasses all particular limited experiences and passes into the absolute mystery who is called God-Father? Or, has there been an arrested development in which finite being has been given absolute status? Thus idolized, the finite would have been substituted for God. In this view death is not an isolated moment, the moment of the medical exit. Rather, death is the horizon within which personal human history is able to become and to become finally valid. Through death it is able to achieve its true identity. As we saw earlier, Jesus had to rise from the dead. Here it is evident that Jesus also had to die. Otherwise his human identity would never have been achieved.

Why is fulfillment through death possible? Because the human being is not only nature but also person. Death also has a natural and a personal dimension. As nature it comes from outside and is imposed upon human beings. It is truly an unavoidable limit experience. However, there is also a personal dimension to the act of death. Dying is the means whereby the human being finally and irrevocably takes his stand for or against God. It is the moment of truth. Will he live truly or falsely—forever? This is possible precisely because of the unlimited transcendence which the transcendental method has been able to discover by reflecting on and analyzing the knowing and choosing acts of the human being. Once more the critical importance of the human being as the one who transcends limits is clearly seen. Even nothingness is not really a limit. "And were we to try to establish a boundary for this seemingly empty horizon of our consciousness, we would again have already surpassed (transcended) it in the very act of positing it. The horizon of the spirit's free activity is boundless" (XIII, 234).

Were this not the case, death would be a passive happening. Inflicted upon the human being from without, it would be simple annihilation of the person. However, since there is a beyond, dying is not merely an event of nature which is pre-given and forced upon the human being. Death is not the last moment of historical existence but the first moment of expanded existence which flows from the personal consummation of historical existence. This moment of truth is not restricted to the final moment; it is a dimension (an existential) of the human being's entire life. It is the manner in which the free, finite human being reacts to his finitude. Traditionally, death has been regarded as the finalizing of the fundamental option for or against God. This is quite acceptable, as long as this finalizing is not restricted to the moment of biological dissolution. Precisely when such a finalizing decision is made in the real history of a human being cannot be pinpointed. Neither the physical condition of the dying nor philosophy and theology nor revelation demand that this finalization coincide chronologically with the medical exit. Rahner has steadily refused to have his position identified with that of Boros, who at least seems to locate the total decision for or against God, which is death, precisely in the moment of the medical-biological exit (most recently, XIII, 273).

Of course, this "last moment" does retain a sort of quasi-sacramental character. In this moment the final graced decision for God receives an unsurpassable spatio-temporal visibility. In death the personal decision receives historical status and cosmic certification. In its essence, though, dying-death is a lifelong letting go. It is the process of letting go of oneself, of one's actions and achievements, of all finitudes which could be mistaken for the absolute, until one finally lets go into that "night in which no one can work anymore" (XIII, 277). One cannot because one need not. Historical working has been consummated.

This does not mean that the human being's relationship with the material world is simply terminated, although the definition of death as "separation of the soul from the body" tends to give this false impression. Since the soul is the substantial form of the body, the human being cannot simply become immaterial. In death the soul does not become acosmic but pancosmic. The historically achieved and finalized human being can henceforth assume a greater role in the unifying and "spiritualizing" of the world.[16] According to Jesus, death does not lead to the abandonment of the world, but to its resurrection and transfiguration. Likewise, in its innermost essence dying is human participation in that transcendental experience of Jesus whereby he constantly referred himself to the will of his Father. The moment of death is the final moment of dying. As such it is participation in Jesus' final "Father into your hands I commit my spirit" (Luke 23:46). Had Jesus spoken Rahnerian, the text would read "Absolute, gracious mystery, into the apeiron of your absolute transcendence my graced spirit in the world now finally, fully, and irrevocably transcends."

Transcendental or Praxis

Because of his method of transcendental reflection Rahner has been accused of abandoning suffering history. Because of his theological anthropology he has been accused of excessively privatizing Christianity. Thus, continues the accusation, he has betrayed suffering humanity with a premature, unreal reconciliation of social and historical contradictions. In the words of his former student, J. B. Metz, theology like Rahner's

> causes those historical contradictions and antagonisms, through which historical experience lives sufferingly and in which the historical subject constitutes itself, to disappear into a precipitate, conceptually asserted "transcendental experience" which is really devoid of reality.

Thus, suffering humanity is said to be delivered over to continual oppression "in which one can't be orthodox (in one's faith). Here consoling is no longer acceptable, here there must also be healing. Here the conditions of living themselves must be transformed."[17]

This is typical of the objections made by political and liberation theology against Rahner's theology. Liberation theology levies basically the same accusations against political theology. Premature and historically unreal reconciliation is a frequent accusation which Ernst Bloch and the Frankfurt School of Critical Theory make, especially against Hegel. Their influence on political and liberation theologians is widely recognized. The latter's application of this criticism to Rahner is more a matter of assertion than demonstration. While political and liberation theologians rightly proclaim that theology should be related to the real world, their own performance does not manifest a superior *praxis* in any way. Their own practice exposes their critique of Rahner's theologizing to be naïve at best.

Rahner himself has always regarded good Judeo-Christian theology as such to be politically and socially critical. Good Christian theology always relativizes all merely finite being — or at least it should. In fact, "the true radicalism of theology can only be the constantly renewed destruction of an idol which has taken the place of God" (VIII, 165; IX, 574-583).

That Rahner's theology offers no practical plans for social, economic and political reform is consistent with his position that theology and the church hierarchy as such have no specific expertise in such matters. In any case, his theology would not suffer in comparison with his praxis critics in this regard. Their praxis is hardly practical. Rahner does not reject political and liberation theology, although he finds deficiencies in them. He correctly points out, above all,

> that these theologies themselves cannot do without transcendental-speculative considerations and historical material. Beyond that passionate proclamation of their own formal essence, they must also work theologically, in common with traditional theology (XIV, 61).

Neither does Rahner simply dismiss Marxist secular humanist and futurological utopian thinkers. He does admonish them to be aware of past historical social failures and the omnipresent ontological failure of personal death. Of course, Rahner does assert an absolute future, God. This absolute future is already explicitly present in history through Christianity. This explicit Christianity not only embraces and heals failed human transcendence, but also mediates this wounded humanity to the true classless society of peace and justice in the eschatological kingdom of God. This kingdom remains forever the most severe critique of all historical human pretensions to absoluteness.

The resurrection and kingdom of God, as the absolute victories over human failure and injustice, do not excuse but impel one to be involved in the history of this world. Because of the incarnation this world's history is the history of not only human transcendence but also of divine transcendence. How human involvement in history is to happen and be structured is the concern of ethics. Although the quantity and quality of Rahner's ethical publications surprise some, his ethical interest is a consistent part of his entire theological enterprise. How the graced historical transcendence of human being actually happens and creates its own history as well as the whole world is the concern of ethics. For Rahner ethics has a threefold dimension—philosphical, theological, existential/*existentiell*. The first two describe a human being precisely insofar as he or she is an entirely unique person, uniquely constituted by a particular call or vocation from God. There is a pre-given dimension to human being which is not only cultural but also cosmic and biological. This pre-given constitutes the context in which all human beings make their personal choices and thus create their history. The human person is not pure person but is also nature. And this nature must be respected: It is *beyond* the power of any individual human being as well as humanity itself.

Rahner finds situation ethics unacceptable. It is an exaggerated existentialism which ultimately equates being with human being. It is really a form of idolatry which absolutizes individual human beings by reducing being as such to the being of their particular situation. Intended to heighten human dignity, situation ethics ends, like all idolatries, by demeaning humanity. It deems the person incapable of and dispenses him or her from the common existentials of human being and behavior. The kernel of truth in situation ethics is developed in what Rahner calls existential ethics, in which he tries to steer a middle course between two extremes. The first regards the human being as merely one more homogeneous part of the physical cosmic universe. The second totally disregards the material, bodily dimension of human being. It removes a person from the cosmos and makes one pure spirit or subject. The first takes away all freedom from the human being. The second makes the person into absolute freedom, which effectively negates possible freedom as well as the first. Rahner's own course is steered between these two. It was already hinted in the title of his philosophy dissertation—the human being is *Spirit in the World.*

The Ignatian parentage of Rahner's existential ethics is apparent in *The Dynamic Element in the Church,* whose third chapter is entitled "The Logic of Concrete Individual Knowledge in Ignatius of Loyola." Behind and at the base of each unique human "thou" is the specific, concrete call of God. Christian logic of existential decision, discernment of spirits, and election are the Ignatian terms which describe the process whereby God's particular summons is discovered by each unique human person. Indeed, in this call is situated precisely his or her existential dignity and uniqueness. Existential ethics describes the duty and process of discovering precisely that which God wants me to be and do. It finds the "secular" task in which my mediated immediacy to God is to be lived. In a word, existential ethics establishes my unique situation in God's graced world.

Fortunately, Rahner is fascinated by the mystery of God, not by sin. For him ethics is only secondarily concerned with sin. Existential ethics enables one to know God's will. One's refusal to live this will is also one's sin. In more philosophical language, sin describes human transcendence which absolutizes itself at some historical point. It closes itself to further transcending, thus idolizing that point. Virtue describes continued openness and response to the call of absolute transcendence in history. In a sense, sin is basically impatience with history. It is either despair, in which the finite world is totally rejected, or it is presumption, in which a particular stage of the finite world is absolutized. In Ignatian language, sin is the refusal to recognize that God is always the greater (*Deus semper maior*). If this refusal of continuing transcendence into God is done with fully personal intensity, one speaks of a grave sin. Were this to perdure until death, one would speak of mortal sin and damnation. Although legitimate in itself, the distinction between grave and venial matter in the sinful act must be used with caution. It is thoroughly possible that grave closure to further transcendence could occur in an act which would not be considered all that important in itself.

Sin is the anxious shutting off of further transcending and the consequent imprisonment of human being in any given here and now. Virtue is continued open-ended transcending and is grounded in a fundamental human existential which Rahner calls *Urvertrauen* or *Grundvertrauen*. Rahner often uses these two words to describe the rock bottom of human and Christian living. *Vertrauen* means "trust." *Ur* means "original," "originating," "primal." *Grund* means "fundamental," "the very foundation." Together they describe the original, fundamental "and ultimate trust and confidence in the meaningfulness of human existence, in the possibility of a complete, all-embracing and final salvation" (X, 287). All subsequent Christianity—church, Bible, virtue, martyrdom, social action—is the concrete articulation of this trust in the various circumstances of history.

It is also known as courage. Today courage is an epochal key concept for humanity. "Courage is the hope that is decision, doing and daring. Without these, hope would not really be hope." In fact, if this hopeful courage is "radical enough, it is already that which Christian theology means by faith in the strict sense." Courage is difficult to define because it is not a particular event in a human being's life, but is the whole life as it is lived. It is not courage for only this or that particular, explicit goal, but is really "the courage to be oneself in the totality of human reality." In our own particular age when human being seems to be threatened with self-destruction and meaninglessness, courage is a key concept. It is a most fitting term to describe that "fundamental human-Christian living of one's own being" which the past has traditionally described by the key concepts of "faith, hope and charity" (XIII, 256). Further specifications about the daily living of this trust-courage are described in books about moral and ascetical-mystical theology as well as the lives of the saints. Old distinctions between natural and supernatural virtues are not very important in Rahner's theology. In a graced universe all virtues are "gifts . . . through them you will be able to share the divine nature and . . . [add] goodness to the faith that you have" (2 Peter 1:4-5).

Love of God and Neighbor

Although love of God and love of neighbor are not identical, in the loving of God and neighbor we have what Rahner calls

> a perichoresis of the conditions requisite for and operative in both (loves). In its very origin and source all radical, selfless love of neighbor always reaches God too. Later theoretical reflection may reveal that I must also say that love of God is more important. That is true, and it is certainly something I have never denied.[18]

This love of neighbor is not a "private, individualistic" affair. It does not make Christians "introverted and withdrawn" (VIII, 227). Because the world is the one creation of the one God, every encounter with an individual human being is simultaneously an encounter with all humanity. In this sense all brotherly love is also necessarily political. How this political dimension of brotherly love becomes really practical depends on the existential situation and particular talents of the individual.

The relationship between the love of God and the love of humans is such that one's fellow human being is really one's neighbor. That is the meaning of the Parable of the Good Samaritan. However, one's fellow human being is even more than neighbor. According to the teaching and example of Jesus, he is also one's brother or sister. Because of the mutuality of love of God and humanity, one's human brother is also a sacrament of the encounter of humanity with God. God is truly mediated and revealed in and by this fellow human being. Once again we emphasize that this does not assert identity between God and humanity. It only asserts that the relationship between divine and human being is so intimate that in the experience of one's human brother one can also experience God. This is not because the human can compel the divine. It is because the generous God freely communicates himself to the not-godly. The result is that all created being is revelation of and communion with the Creator.

This sacramental ontology is the basis for Rahner's theology of the church and the sacraments—indeed, of Christology itself. Jesus is the sacrament of God. That is, the corporeal, historical Jesus is both the cause and sign of God's grace in the world. Jesus is the presence of God in the world. This does not require that God's presence be limited to the historical Jesus. That is why we say that Jesus is *the* sacrament of grace. He reveals most intensely what God, the universal savior, is doing in and for his entire creation. As Jesus is the sacrament of God, so is the church the sacrament of Jesus. The church is the cause and sign of Jesus' continued presence in the later history of the world. The relationship between Jesus and grace is continued in the church. The church is truly the cause and sign of grace. But grace is not limited to the historical church. And church and salvation do not simply coincide.

The sacraments illustrate how the Bible can be the sacred Scripture and not just another religious book. Neither sacraments nor Scripture is superstition or magic. They do not make God do anything. They are, rather, the temporal and spatial presence, the here and now appearance of what God is already and always doing. All this is possible, as we saw earlier, because all being, divine and human, is symbolic. Being truly expresses itself and makes itself present in the "other." In the relationship between God and the world this "other" is preeminently Jesus, the Incarnate Word of God. But, as we have also seen, Jesus is not to be thought of in individualistic terms. As the perfect encounter of the human and divine, he is the perfect sacrament—making God present to us and us present to God. Hence, for Rahner, the founding of the church and the institution of the sacraments by Christ are not insoluble theological dilemmas. Like Jesus himself, the church and the sacraments are the objectifications of the human experience of God in time and space. Jesus is the personal objectification of this experience. The church is the tradition of this objectification throughout time and space. Like Jesus, the church does not limit God's grace but reveals it to be really present. The church does not hold grace captive within its empirical boundaries but, like Christ, it strikingly reveals that there is grace. The church is not the Lord of grace, but its servant. Not the church, but the grace which it mediates signfully is the important thing. One of Rahner's greatest achievements has been to emphasize the presence of this grace everywhere. He speaks of the mysticism of everyday life precisely because grace is not limited to isolated "mystical moments." It is everywhere.

Prayer

Everyday lived grace is paramount. In this everyday lived grace, prayer is paramount. In one sense, prayer is easy. Our graced lives themselves are already orientation to, acceptance of, and commitment to God. However, this unthematic, preconceptual prayer has a dynamism of its own which becomes explicitly present in the human consciousness in what we customarily call prayers or praying.

Obviously such an understanding is perfectly at home in Rahner's sacramental ontology. And it is not at all surprising that his first published article was on the need for prayer.[19] Early in his career Rahner summed up his theology of humanity in general and prayer in particular. We repeat, from a prayer to the "God of Knowledge": "You have grasped me (*ergriffen*), I have not comprehended you (*begriffen*). You have transformed my being in its deepest roots and earliest origins. You have given to me a sharing in your very being and life."[20] The rest of Rahner's life and theology is the celebration of this divine seizure. Our prayer need not always be directed outwardly to God, since God is not only beyond, but equally present within us. This gracious dialogue between God and humankind in the very depths of concrete, personal human existence is prototypical prayer. What we commonly call *prayer* is the explicit making of this ontological state of being at prayer, which is ours by virtue of the Holy Spirit dwelling in us. So by our very graced being we fulfill St. Paul's exhortation to "pray constantly" (1 Thess. 5:17). Our explicit prayer, whether in word or rite, is the "sacramental" witnessing of our prayer-full being. By grace this has already been transformed into intimate dialogue with God. For Rahner there is no essential conflict between the active and contemplative lives. A "deed may often be a prayer. But prayer is also a deed."[21]

Anonymous Christianity

His understanding of the God-world relationship in Christ enables Rahner to understand graced life as prayer. It also enables him to speak of anonymous Christianity. No other theory of Rahner has provoked such hostile reactions.[22] Hans Urs von Balthasar, who otherwise misrepresents this theory, does correctly note the relationship between the theories of the supernatural existential and anonymous Christianity. However, anonymous Christianity is not merely such a consequence. It is primarily Rahner's attempt to reconcile the universal saving will of God with the unique mediatorship of the man Jesus according to 1 Timothy 2:4. It is secondarily his attempt to explain the teaching of Vatican II.

> In contrast to the customary theology until then (namely, that one could not be an atheist in good will for a long period of time), it allows for the possibility that the saving virtues of faith, hope and charity can also be present in atheists who continue in their atheism (XII, 255).

To regard anonymous Christianity merely as a deduction from the supernatural existential is a serious oversimplification. Can it be other than willful?

Rahner has never insisted on the name "anonymous Christianity," although no better one has been suggested (X, 532). He has, however, insisted on the theory. It is necessary because

the possibility of supernatural salvation and the corresponding saving faith has been acknowledged for non-Christians, even if they do not become Christians. At the same time, this salvation cannot be achieved in simply bypassing God and Jesus Christ. Ultimately it must be theist and Christian salvation—in its origin, history and consummation (XII, 275).

Rahner tries to explain how the relationship between God and the world enables one to enjoy the benefits of Christ, God's absolute presence in the world, even though one's relationship to this Christ is not empirically verified.

The real question is why anyone would object to this theory. The first objection is that the term is inadequate. To this Rahner has regularly responded that the thing is important, not the name. He will gladly accept a "better word" as soon as it is offered. Ernst Jüngel insists that

> in its very essence Christianity is not only not anonymous, it is downright anti-anonymous. The Christian faith not only wants to be recognized by the name of him to whom it owes its existence and continued sustenance, it also wants to be recognized by his name and charged with it.[23]

This is, of course, all well and good. But it does not solve the problem of whether those without this name share in the goods of the name. If not, what happens to these nameless ones? If yes, how is one to describe this phenomenon, which Rahner calls anonymous Christianity? Jüngel suggests "more human human being," Küng "more radical human being."[24] Suffering, as they do from almost terminal vagueness, these can hardly be considered improvements. Nor do they escape at least the possibility of denigrating the dignity of those who are not explicitly Christian—an objection made by these and many other critiques to the term, if not the reality, of anonymous Christianity. At least Rahner's theory makes it clear that the anonymity is not a deficiency in the holiness, dignity, and being of the non-Christians. It is only in the reflective, explicit conceptualizing of the anonymously Christian consciousness. Globally this is not without significance. How significant it might be for any anonymously Christian individual person is not at all clear.[25]

Explicit objection is made that "anonymous Christian" is in fact an insult to the persons so designated, whether it is so intended or not. This objection misses the point entirely. This theory is not a cryptic attempt to make of people what they don't want to be in the first place. In any case, Rahner also speaks of anonymous theists, anonymous Lutherans, anonymous Catholics (X, 500; IX, 183-196; 78). When a famous Japanese philosopher asked him how he would react, if he were called an anonymous Zen Buddhist, Rahner replied:

> Of course from your standpoint you may and you must do so. I could only feel honored by such an interpretation, even if I would nevertheless have to regard it as mistaken, or presuppose that, correctly interpreted, genuine Zen-Buddhist-Being and correctly understood Christian-Being are identical at *that* (ontological) level which is actually and immediately intended by such statements.[26]

Neither is the theory an imperious "we know you better than you know yourselves" imposition on those who are designated anonymous Christians. Nor is it a dishonest attempt to swell the church rolls in an era of declining church attendance. This theory is really an inner-churchly theological statement. It answers the question: Is the good which I enjoy because of my explicit Christian faith also available to the whole of human creation and history, or is it somehow restricted to a few? Furthermore, even Jesus allowed for some kind of anonymously lived relationship to him: " 'Lord, when did we see you . . .?' 'I tell you solemnly, in so far as you neglected to do this to one of the least of these, you neglected to do it to me' " (Matt. 25:39-40).

The final objection comes from Hans Urs von Balthasar. The theory of anonymous Christianity

> implies a relativizing of the objective revelation of God in the biblical event and would sanction the objective religious practices/praxis of other religions as ordinary or extraordinary ways of salvation.[27]

Consequently the Christian is reduced to the merely human. Its missionary mandate is muffled if not annulled. And martyrdom is rendered otiose if not odious.

How von Balthasar reconciles this objection with his own theory and hope for universal salvation can be readily remitted to his own care. With reference to the parables of the Good Samaritan and the last judgment, he has himself written: "Hence, it is not necessary, indeed not even possible, that Christian love should understand whence it comes or whither it goes."[28] Unless such a statement is to be merely a bald assertion, a theory at least like Rahner's anonymous Christianity is necessary. In fact, von Balthasar does find Henri de Lubac's distinction between anonymous Christianity (unacceptable) and anonymous Christians (acceptable) illuminating. Why? Since

> the grace of Christ is operative outside the Church, one may speak of "anonymous Christians" . . . but only through a false deduction could one conclude to a widespread "anonymous Christianity" within humanity, an "implicit Christianity" so to speak.[29]

Rahner himself does not find this distinction helpful. And rightly so. It is a prime example of the carping criticism to which Rahner is subject from certain corners. According to this suggestion, one could have widespread "anonymous Christians" without widespread "anonymous Christianity." After all is said and done, the question remains. Do people other than those who explicitly rejoice in the name "Christian" share in the gifts mediated by and revealed in Jesus Christ? If no, then we don't have the problem we thought we had. If yes, then our problem is to explain how this is possible. That is what Rahner has attempted in the theory known as anonymous Christianity. Whatever may be said about the title, his explanation has not yet been bettered.

The name itself is not all that bad. A friend of Hans Küng recently told me that Küng objected to the theory of anonymous Christianity because Christ (Christianity) is a name and therefore can't be anonymous. Although I cannot vouch for the veracity of the narration, I have no reason to mistrust it. Unfortunately, it betrays the lack of even elementary acquaintance with the dictionary. "Anonymous" means "1. without any name acknowledged; 2. of unknown name; whose name is withheld."[30] Anonymous is not impossible because there is a name. Rather, precisely because there is the name "Christ," there can be anonymous Christianity. Earlier I noted the customary assertion that the theory of "anonymous Christianity is a blatant consequence of Rahner's Christology." I also noted that one can and must equally assert that Rahner's Christology is a clear consequence of his anonymous Christian ontology. I would now like to expand on this.

The question is not only why God became human. It is also how this incarnation affects the very being of humanity and how explicit awareness of this divine-human relationship is significant. The answer is implicit in all our preceding pages. Human being is spirit. It can know and love. It is interpersonal communion and communication. As creature it is also history. Human history is essentially solidarity in both the experienced need for salvation and the received satisfaction of this need. Rahner calls human experience and human history itself "seeking Christology" (XIII, 174, 225). The hypostatic union is the finality and end of this graced quest. "Because the world is *one* world to which God has communicated himself in his Spirit, therefore this intercommunicational world as history has a (one!) consummation and goal, and this is Jesus Christ" (VIII, 232). "In scholastic terms, incarnation and cross are to be understood as the 'final cause' of the universal self-communication of God to the world." The universal communication of the Spirit never happens in mere abstract transcendence, but always in historical mediation. The universal saving will of God is originally

> oriented toward an historical event in which this divine self-communication and its human acceptance become irreversible and historically graspable. All this takes place in what we call the Incarnation, Cross and Resurrection of the divine Word.[31]

This means that all human history, even before and apart from explicit Christianity, is essentially constituted as Christ-ian or Christ-ic. All fully human acts are at least possibly Christ-ly acts. If God seriously and actively wills the salvation of all people and offers them the grace to obtain this salvation, then anonymous Christianity describes what is the case until the history of this saving will and its grace has reached its "fullness of time" and has become fully present to itself. It also means that Jesus is not speaking merely metaphorically in the last judgment scene (Matthew 25:31-46). What you have done to these you have done to me is really, ontologically, literally the case. Certainly, then, we humans can be Godlike when we do good unto others. That is what God does. When, however, in the real order God does good to the other which is our world, then we have Christ. Some already know the very name of Christ. Others do not, at least not yet. But, because some do know this name, they also know that human actions can be anonymously Christian.

Perhaps this manner of speaking would alleviate the fears of some. It emphasizes that anonymous Christianity is not a negative term. It does not refer precisely to people who are not explicit Christians, but does refer precisely to people who are human beings in God's already graced world. The combined theories of the supernatural existential and anonymous Christianity certainly enable us to take seriously what the people of the Old Testament already knew when they heard God saying:

Long before they call I shall answer (Isaiah 65:24).

... I have called you by your name,
conferring a title though you do not know me.
... Though you do not know me, I arm you
that men may know from the rising to the setting of the sun
that, apart from me, all is nothing (Isaiah 45:4-6).

A sermon attributed to St. Augustine asserts: "But already then [in Genesis] Mary was included in Eve; yet it was only when Mary came that we knew who Eve was."[32] There could not be a better description of Rahner's theological method of transcendental reflection on the tradition of the divine revelation which our graced human history already is and whose historical culmination is Jesus the Christ! In him is revealed who we have been from the very beginning.

CHAPTER 3

Sources of
Rahner's Theology

What is the origin of the theology of Karl Rahner? We have already mentioned various sources in the preceding pages. Here we want to give a more orderly presentation. A special reason for this systematic approach is to counter the overemphasis placed on the influence of the Kant-Marechal school of philosophy. Certainly such influence is strongly present. However, as we have seen, even Rahner's method is not primarily beholden to this philosophical source.

Tradition

I think only one word is really adequate to describe the source of Rahner's theology—*tradition*. In earlier days, before he wandered off into political theology, J. B. Metz's first choice to describe Rahner's "theological personality" was

> the affirmation of the tradition: his sense of responsibility for and rootedness in the history of the Church and the faith.... For him the question about the tradition is the question of theology about itself, always according to its own self-understanding in any given age. Thus, for Rahner, theology's living future is mediated out of its own origins. He seeks out the new, not for the sake of modernity, but for the sake of loyalty to theology's historical beginnings.[1]

His brother Hugo found that a text of Irenaeus most aptly described their mutual theological enterprise: "We must love most intimately everything which belongs to the Church and embrace the tradition of the truth" (his translation of *Adv. Haer.* III, 4,1).[2] We have already seen one example of Rahner's devotion to the tradition in regard to the term "person" in trinitarian theology. There has been development in Rahner's theology, but few substantial reversals. His change of mind about monogenism may be the only such reversal, as Karl Lehmann indicates.[3]

Rahner has been accused by Küng and others of being a merely speculative theologian, without sufficient rootedness in historical theology. Yet Rahner's writings include historical studies of both patristic and scholastic authors. Of course, he is not a universal specialist for the history of theology. But, then, neither is anyone else. In the above article Metz speaks of Rahner's "immense historical knowledge." In 1963 Metz was already able to note that this historical background was frequently unappreciated and even simply ignored.

Philosophy and St. Thomas Aquinas

For Rahner the thought of St. Thomas Aquinas has been a privileged source. Of course, as Gerald McCool has pointed out, Rahner does not fit into the Thomist, neo-Thomist or transcendental Thomist mold.[4] Rahner is amazingly familiar with the scholastic theology of recent theological manuals, Thomist or otherwise. One of his great feats has been to rescue the inner meaning of traditional doctrines from the obscurity of these scholastic formulations. However, the theology and philosophy of these scholastic textbooks was not the real influence on Rahner. The real influence was the thought of St. Thomas Aquinas himself. I have indicated this very briefly in my response to McCool in the volume cited above. Here again Rahner did not simply parrot. Rather, Aquinas was truly a source or fountain, from which Rahner creatively developed his own thought.

Although Rahner does not claim to be a professional philosopher, he does claim to have a *Heidenrespekt* for philosophy (XII, 599). The German *Heiden* means not only "heathen," but also "enormous," "mortal." It would not be entirely incorrect to translate it as an "almost superstitious respect for philosophy." This indicates how great a presence philosophical thinking and reflecting have in Rahner's theology. Christian faith—not philosophy—is his starting point. It is his rigorous and deep philosophizing that enables him to understand and explain this faith so well. The range of Rahner's knowledge of philosophy is impressive. One must keep in mind that he did prepare for a career as a professor of philosophy. Rahner's protests about "feeling very much dumber now" than when he began teaching forty years ago and of being a "dilettante" must also be kept in the proper perspective (XII, 21, 603). His philosophical proclivity prompts great expectations in regard to what can be called scientific or strict knowledge. The contemporary knowledge explosion makes it very difficult to become an expert specialist. How much more difficult, if not impossible, is the ideal of the universal genius—even scholar. It is in this context that we must understand Rahner's seeming skepticism about a modern thinker's ability to be a systematic theologian.

Scripture

Rahner's declaration that he is not an expert in scriptural studies must also be greeted with the same caution. In his review of *Foundations*, Harvey Egan explicitly states what Rahner's students have always known: "His exegetical mastery and his overall *sense* of Scripture are awesome, as the Karl Rahner-Wilhelm Thüsing volume to cite only one of many possible examples, *(Christologie-systematisch und exegetisch*, [Freiburg: Herder, 1972]), clearly indicates."[5] The value of this overall sense of Scripture is evident in Rahner's discussion of problems requiring intensive scriptural argumentation. A good example is provided by Francis Fiorenza's comparison of Rahner's and Küng's discussion of the foundation of the church by Christ.[6] Although the quantity of exegetical references in Küng is much greater, it is also clear that Rahner's position is scripturally and exegetically more responsible and reliable. The remark Leo Bakker makes about Rahner's exegesis of the writings of Ignatius of Loyola is also applicable to his biblical studies: "Rahner wrote, so to speak, theologically straight on exegetically crooked lines."[7]

Signs of the Times

An important source for Rahner's theology has been the signs of the times. In spite of his great love of philosophy, he has written:

> In the future, theology's key partner-in-dialogue, to which it will have to relate its 'philosophising' in the sense we have adumbrated, will no longer be philosophy in the traditional sense at all. It will be the 'unphilosophical' pluralistic sciences and the kind of understanding of existence which they promote either

directly or indirectly. At least in the concrete situation deter-
mined by the cultural, intellectual, social and natural sciences,
it is science, no longer mediated by philosophy, which constitutes theology's partner-in-dialogue (VIII, 83).

Rahner's bibliography indicates that his attentiveness to the signs
of the times has ranged from poets to novelists to natural scientists,
from the "heavy" Martin Heidegger to the "fluffy" Francoise Sagan.

Opponents of both Rahner and Teilhard de Chardin are fond of
linking them, thereby, it is hoped, refuting both with one blow.
Others link them for various reasons and motives. Whatever the precise influence Teilhard had on Rahner, it was certainly later than earlier, lesser than greater. In any case, George Lindbeck's judgment
remains reliable:

> Teilhard de Chardin is doubtless the most famous representa-
> tive of a realistically futuristic eschatological interpretation of
> the modern world view, but one finds basically the same vision
> developed in a far more theologically responsible way in Karl
> Rahner, for example.[8]

Under "signs of the times" I would also include a source that is
generally overlooked but which is present in Rahner's theological experience as well as in that of many of the most influential theologians
of his generation. I refer to the experience of World War II. I mean
not only the general misery and suffering everyone experienced
which, of course, was also of crucial importance. However, for
Rahner and his fellow theologians the interruption of their academic
careers was critical. They were literally driven out of their university
ivory towers. Only professors who were totally academic dinosaurs
could have escaped sharing in the specific signs of the times. For
some theologians—including, I think, Rahner—this experience was not
only an occasion but a source of their theologizing. His concern for
the *Glaubensnot* of the contemporary person shows it. The importance of experience for Rahner's theology is strikingly manifest in the
next source we shall consider.

Mystics and Ignatius of Loyola

By far the most overlooked source of Rahner's thought has been
the influence of the mystics, especially the mystical experience of

Ignatius of Loyola. Any hesitation about this had to be eliminated by one of Rahner's latest books. In *Ignatius of Loyola* Rahner plays the role of the founder of his own religious order. The book is subtitled "Ignatius of Loyola Speaks to a Modern Jesuit." The first chapter is entitled "The Direct Experience of God." There is no doubt that Rahner is speaking in the person of Ignatius. There is equally no doubt that Rahner is speaking in the person of Karl Rahner. From the very beginning of his theological career Rahner has told us this.

As we saw in Chapter One, Rahner has insisted on the importance of the spiritual, pious, devotional, mystical works among his writings. Scholars have tended to bypass his admonitions about these writings and the writings themselves—to their own disadvantage. Even Anne Carr's *The Theological Method of Karl Rahner* is not as good as it could easily have been. Her select bibliography lists hardly any of Rahner's devotional writings. The word "select" will not afford comfort. Had they played a greater role, she would have been much less inclined to such statements as "despite apparently sharp discontinuities, between the 'early' and the 'later' Rahner" and, "His later work radically shifts to an investigation of the new *experience* of the subject of revelation in an increasingly secular context."[9] Of course, the context is increasingly secular. That the world has become increasingly de-Christianized culturally is a refrain in the Rahnerian corpus. But the experience of the believing subject has always been the topic of Rahner's investigations. Furthermore, however new the cultural context, the ontological experience and question remain constant. Thus, she correctly notes the general continuity in Rahner's theological development. Critical, however, for this continuity is the rootedness of Rahner's theology in mystical experience. This mystical experience is twofold. It is, first of all, Rahner's own immediate, personal religious experience. It is also the experience of others as this is mediated through the history of the mystical theological tradition. Rahner's book on *Ignatius of Loyola* allows no doubt that these two mystical sources are complementary.

As early as 1956 he had explicity left no doubt about the Ignatian dimension of his theology:

This fundamental formula of Ignatian spirituality was doubtless rooted in his mystical experience. It is, in fact, the attempt of the mystic to translate his experience for others and make them share in his grace, as Nadal once said.[10]

Rahner basically agrees with Origen: "Every knowledge of God is more or less mystical, although it is not necessary to postulate a genuine mystical knowldge in all such cases" (XII, 128). For Rahner, "tomorrow's religious person (the pious one) will be a 'mystic' who has 'experienced' something, or he won't be at all" (VII, 22). In addition to Ignatius of Loyola, John of the Cross, Theresa of Avila, Bonaventure, and many others have influenced him. He insists that this mystical experience need not be extraordinary. It does not imply visions, ecstasy, or any other parapsychological phenomena. He delights in speaking of the "mysticism of everyday life," which is possible because of the Ignatian principle of "finding God in all things" (XIII, 243-245). In our graced world

> faith means that the human being freely embraces the flow of everyday life without selfish compromise. Thus, in his seemingly secular weekday existence the human being experiences that even his daily life is already borne along and carried by God (X, 417.)

For this reason theology is to be a "mystagogy of the mysticism of everyday life" (XIV, 236). Rahner's own best contribution to this mystagogy or initiation to the experience of God in everyday life is in two essays entitled "Experiencing the Spirit" and "Faith as Courage."[11]

The mystical experience of God is not restricted to everyday life, but is also intensely present in the sacraments. Even these celebrations do not, however, eliminate the hiddenness of God. Once again we see the influence of

> St. Thomas Aquinas [who] is the mystic of the adoration of the mystery . . . where he (the human being) no longer grasps (comprehends; *begreift*), but is grasped (comprehended; *ergriffen*), where he no longer reasons, but adores, where he no longer conquers, but is encompassed. The "Adoro te devote, *latens* Deitas, quae sub his figuris latitas" must . . . be the innermost principle of all theological thinking and knowing.[12]

The Latin is the title and beginning of a hymn composed by Aquinas for the feast of Corpus Christi. This feast is in honor of Christ truly present in the bread and wine of the Eucharist. The Latin means "I adore you devoutly, O hidden Godhead. You lie beneath these figures or symbols [of bread and wine]."

This quotation from Rahner was written in 1961, about the middle of his career. But we are certainly reminded of the so-called early Rahner of 1938: "You have seized (grasped, comprehended; *ergriffen*) me; I have not seized (comprehended; *begriffen*) you."[13] Are we not equally reminded of the so-called later Rahner of 1973, who also cites the *Adoro Te* as he writes:

> We must let ourselves fall into the incomprehensibility [of God] as the true fulfillment and happiness. This daring venture, itself beyond understanding, sweeps aside all questions. Usually called the adoring love of God, it alone allows the darkness to be light. This letting oneself fall is both destiny and deed in one, hence free and voluntary.[14]

"Destiny" translates *Geschick*, a complicated word, especially in Heidegger's usage. Early on the word meant the common fortune of human beings. Later on its etymological possibilities are more fully developed. It then connotes sending, history, fortune, coming to pass, event, a com-mitting (by a person). This is another good example of how difficult it is to translate Rahner as well as a good example of how he uses Heidegger's thought and vocabulary. He does not simply parrot or impose Heideggerian concepts on the Christian tradition. Rather, through them he is able to mediate the experience and tradition of Christianity to a new generation. This new generation may think in a different cultural manner than previous generations. Nevertheless, its fundamental ontological questing remains the same. We cannot escape the question of being for we cannot escape the question of meaning. Since we can escape neither, we cannot escape the question of God. That is the horizon within which all of Rahner's theologizing is done.

Heidegger and Przywara

Are there no contemporary teachers who can be included in the sources of theology? It would seem not. In an interview on his seventy-fifth birthday, Rahner remarked that "even among such people, I would not really say that I have met the great master to whom alone, in one way or another, I was bound in blazing discipleship."[15] Here is, then, a fitting place to comment on the influence of Martin Heidegger on Rahner. In contrast to those who have wished to make Rahner a Heideggerian, he has protested at least as early as 1967 that "perhaps Dr. Roberts overestimates this latter influence [Heidegger] somewhat."[16] In the above interview, he also says, "But if, in fact, I ask myself, for example, whether Heidegger exercised a great influence on me, then I would say that I am not exactly sure." However, in a television interview Rahner did designate Heidegger as the "one" whom he "can revere (as his) teacher." He adds, and this, I think, is the precise influence of Heidegger on Rahner:

> and precisely this one thing did he thoroughly teach us: that in all and everything we can and must search out that ineffable mystery which rules over us and disposes our being—still, and indeed, even when and if we can hardly name it with words.[17]

One more influence must also be noted by name, again at Rahner's own behest, Erich Przywara. Also a Jesuit, it is quite possible that he has been the single most influential force in the twentieth century renewal of Catholic theology and philosophy. This is certainly the case for Germany. While he and his thought remain virtually unknown outside German-speaking circles, his influence has been mediated through theologians like Rahner and von Balthasar. Rahner notes explicitly that "he has been closely associated with him for a good forty years." Przywara's influence was general and specific. In general his thought is an excellent illustration of the role philosophy plays in theology. For Rahner he also provided an altogether specific service. He is the "first one who made Ignatius of Loyola properly understood in the history of Christian thought and spirituality and erased the baroque scholastic image under which he had been hidden."[18] For Rahner this meant that Ignatius and his spirituality were not primarily moralistic and ascetic, but were primarily metaphysical and mystical. And thus they could be true sources of true theologizing.

If Rahner learned to think of humanity as mystery in a phenomenological, anthropological manner from Heidegger, he learned how to transform this into an ontological anthropology from Przywara and his profound understanding of the analogy of being.

Conclusion

All told, the primary source of Rahner's thought is not philosophy. Certainly not Kant, Marechal, or Heidegger, nor even Aquinas or Przywara. The only adequate description of a single source would have to be the Catholic Christian tradition. Within this tradition special attention must be paid to the mystical, experiential tradition, especially that of Ignatius of Loyola.

This obvious rootedness of Rahner's theology is confirmed by his uncharacteristic touchiness in response to Leo O'Donovan's question in the above interview: "Would you say that Ignatius of Loyola has molded your own religious experience?" Rahner replied:

> Naturally, I don't want to say all too much about that, because it isn't really anybody else's business. . . . But I think that the spirituality of Ignatius himself, which one learned through the practice of prayer and religious formation, was more significant for me than all learned philosophy and theology.

CHAPTER 4

Critique

As with all famous people, Rahner is subject to the most varied criticisms. Some have already been discussed. Often enough these criticisms counter each other. For some he has written too much, studied too little. For others he has not written enough—at least on their favorite topics. If he didn't say everything right away, he is superficial and narrow. If he develops an idea over a period of time, we are cautioned about discontinuity in his thought. He is also blamed for disciples whose extrapolations he has explicitly disclaimed.

Hans Urs von Balthasar, both an admirer and an opponent of Rahner, suggests that *"es gibt viele* Karl Rahner!" ("There are many Karl Rahners!")[1] Meant as a caution, this declaration is a commendation. It acknowledges the wide-ranging interests of Rahner's theologizing. Balthasar also bemoans Rahner's "intrepid projects" [because they] "are often one-sided and not mutually coordinated." Liberation theologians bemoan the universalist balance of traditional continental theologians like Rahner, who are presumed to be paralyzed, inactive, and thus irrelevant in the real suffering and exploited world. During all this Rahner is defending the legitimacy of theological one-sidedness, which he finds was already operative in Thomas Aquinas.[2]

Knowing and Intersubjectivity

It is often said that Rahner is unduly preoccupied with knowledge and the act of knowing. But, as Andrew Tallon has noted, one must start somewhere. One cannot do everything all at once. Rahner's early works did not exclude but were clearly open to and foundational for the later, more extensive development of personal and interpersonal categories.[3]

Especially Alexander Gerken and Eberhard Simons have criticized the lack of intersubjectivity in Rahner's writings. They have urged a dialogic theology to replace Rahner's transcendental theology. Their critique is not generally regarded as cogent. Simons' interpretation of the I-Thou relationship is so hyper-personalist that it cannot claim serious consideration as a description of human or divine being. In response to these two critics, Rahner has insisted that human being, as historical, knowing, choosing, is always inter-subjective. As personal it can only be inter-personal. For example, in 1952 he emphasized that

> the human personality cannot be adequately lived or explained as absolute interiority. It needs a certain exterior space for its existence and development. This is essential. Withdrawal into the purely private, into the conscience within, into the sacristy is contrary to the essence and nature of the human being (II, 252).

Rahner does not claim that this dimension of human being is fully developed in each one of his publications. However, he rightly rejects the accusations that his theology is so transcendentally individualistic that the inter-subjective dimension is absent. Furthermore, the very title of Simons' book on Rahner, *Philosophy of Revelation*, is seriously misleading. Rahner's intent has never been a philosophy of revelation. In the Christian tradition, which already claims a supernatural revelation, his concern has been a "philosophy" of a possible hearing of such a revelation. Simons has written: "Thus Being *(Sein)* is given, according to *Hearers of the Word, only* as the condition of the possibility of objective knowledge; it is not, however, itself objectively *(gegenständlich)* given" (emphasis mine).[4] Such a comment in regard to Rahner deserves but the briefest attention.

Language and Style

Rahner's language and style are often criticized. In a review of *Foundations* James Mackey was "stricken . . . by the turgid germanic prose and the convoluted thought patterns. The book is virtually unreadable . . . except [by] those . . . infected with similar stylistic and conceptual views."[5] Mackey, obviously sparsely published, finally gets to the point: "The book would also be unnecessary if American publishers reduced their dependence on translations and realized that theological thought of equal status is regularly produced for them at home." The *odium theologicum* is rivalled only by the *invidia theo-*

logorum. Mackey suggests that his review is "both ungracious and unwise." It is because it clearly misses the intent of the book. The infelicitous *Foundations* in the title of the translation may have abetted his error. This technical philosophical term is not at all descriptive of Rahner's intent. I have been given to understand (*not* by the translator himself) that this title is not the responsibility of the translator. In any case, it is misleading. However, one would assume that Mackey, for whom "the argument of the book is simple enough," would have been able to recognize this discrepancy. After all, the original German title is given on the copyright page.

In any case, is the argument all that simple? It obviously eluded Mackey. Rahner does not "threaten them [prominent philosophers from Hegel to Sartre] with the ultimate emptiness of a human horizon." Rather, he shows that, however full or empty, neither the human horizon nor its contents is possible without that which the Christian tradition and all humanity have called God. The very ineptness of this review supports the assertion that there is an essential coherence between Rahner's thought and his particular language/style. Since this style is oral, certain implications and emphases in Rahner's writings can elude those who have not been hearers of his lectures. In defense of Rahner's style and thought, we may well recall the words of an ancient master. Aristotle had already acknowledged that "our discussion will be adequate if it has as much clearness as the subject matter admits of, for precision is not to be sought for alike in all discussions."[6] We should also note that in 1973 Rahner received the Sigmund Freud Award for Scientific (*wissenschaftliche*) Prose. This award acknowledged the influence of his language, not only for theology but also for the other humanities. Short sentences and semantic simplicity may very well have their own value. They do not, fortunately, exhaust the capacities of the human mind and pen.

The Cross and Resurrection

Complaint is also lodged against the insufficiency of Rahner's theology of the cross. Nevertheless, as Rahner notes, Anselm Grün has been able to write a doctoral dissertation on the subject.[7] Perhaps Rahner's realistically but not pessimistically modest understanding of "human potential" enabled him early on to avoid that human hybris which comes crashing down in the face of the cross. His entire theology and ontology of human being insist that its innermost essence is a letting go, a surrendering of self into the gracious mystery beyond. This better starting point does not require Rahner to evacuate the cross of its unique and crucial meaning. It may, however, serve him well in avoiding that traumatic fascination that tends to understand the cross as transforming God from wrath to forgiveness. Not only Rahner's faith, but his theology as well, knows that the cross does not transform God from wrath to forgiveness (XII, 261). Rather, it reveals him to be forgiveness. In any case, Rahner has long insisted that human transcendence is historical. Human being, even as transcendent, happens precisely in history. As truly human in our real world, Jesus is not able to avoid the cross of death, whether this be by crucifixion or otherwise.

Recently I was informed of another complaint: Rahner's theology of the resurrection is inadequate, because Rahner is so dependent on Heidegger's philosophy. Heidegger's philosophy does not enable an adequte theology of the resurrection. The adequate response to such a complaint transcends polite language. I include it here to illustrate how picky the critique of Rahner can be. Rahner's theology of the resurrection, whether Christ's or Christian's, may indeed be inadequate—but not because he is a Heideggerian. For Rahner's theology the resurrection is especially difficult. Resurrection means that the humanly lived history of grace is received into the finally and eternally validating but still incomprehensible embrace of the absolute divine transcendence. I am not aware that any human adequacy has notably thrived in the explanation of such considerations.

Transcendental

The most persistent criticism of Rahner can be summed up in the word *transcendental*. Rahner's theology is accused of being transcendental and therefore untrue to Christianity. It betrays either the history of Christianity or the supernatural gratuity of its grace and revelation. In various ways this charge has been levelled by Hans Küng, Leo Scheffczyk, and Hans Urs von Balthasar—at first glance an unlikely theological triangle.

Küng has coupled this accusation with his others, namely that

Rahner's theology is innocent of historical and exegetical sophistication. His attempt to refute Rahner by this transcendental accusation is as vain as the other two. It must be as willful. As late as 1980 Küng still spoke of "the speculative-transcendental mediation of Karl Rahner."[8] To speak of Rahner's method as transcendental is questionable enough. To describe it as precisely "speculative-transcendental" is not only questionable, but venal. Can it be anything but a ploy to convict him by association? "Speculative-transcendental" must inevitably evoke the spectre of absolute German idealism, its deduction of everything from some abstract idea of pure being, its disdain of everything historical. This is in no wise what Rahner does. He has often and vigorously protested against such descriptions. Küng himself has endured misreadings of his own books. Why he would want to persist in such a crass misinterpretation and misrepresentation of Rahner's theology is not at all clear. One must certainly take into account the academic rivalry and combat in which German professors have traditionally revelled. One need only recall Ernst Käsemann's metaphor of the *Kleinkriege*—the guerilla or mini-wars—of biblical specialists. Küng need not agree with Rahner. And Rahner may be right or wrong. But it is at best unseemly to persist in mislabelling his theology "transcendental speculative"—especially on the part of the author of a book entitled *Truthfulness*.

According to some, Rahner's transcendental-anthropological reflection does not allow full value to the supernatural dimension and explicit Christic character of the Christian revelation and grace. Christianity is reduced to humanism. It is not only formally, but *materially* anthropocentric. Rahner is found guilty of theological reductionism. That this is not the case has often been the burden of Rahner's writings as well as of others. Nevertheless, this criticism continues. It is resumed most succinctly by Leo Scheffczyk in his review of *Foundations*.[9] He asserts that Rahner's transcendental approach is at least wounded, if not simply executed, by Teilhard's evolutionary thought. Why? Because Teilhard's purely *a posteriori* approach, with its purely categorical, temporal-empirical thinking, achieves the same Christology as Rahner's transcendental deduction. That this is not the case is clear from George Lindbeck's comments. Furthermore, would Rahner find anything "purely categorical," especially in the present graced world? Scheffczyk continues by asserting that "in any case, Rahner's thought is less concerned with a clarification of the Incarnation *(Menschwerdung)* of God than with the Divinization of man *(Gottwerdung)."* The mutuality of the divine and human in Christ and Christianity would certainly prompt Rahner to wonder how this could be a problem. Scheffczyk's complaint is really a compliment, unintended, but nonetheless clearly acceptable. It is a clear indication that Rahner's theology is not so narrowly Western-Latin that it cannot enjoy the Eastern emphasis on the divinization of the person *(theiosis)*. Later Scheffczyk asserts that

> one cannot adore divine mystery which is indissolubly fastened *(verknupft)* to the transcendentality of human beings, not even then when it explicitates itself in historical deeds. By definition, these cannot bring forth more than what is already present implicitly and unreflexibly.

The adequate response to this total misperception of Rahner's theology was suggested by one of my colleagues: "Nonsense!" It is true that only that can be brought forth which is already implicitly present. But Scheffczyk precisely perverts Rahner's procedure. The present categorical state of affairs only represents what the transcendent God has chosen to do in the past and present. It does not establish what God can do simply or in the future. Neither does transcendental analysis or reflection determine what God can do. Rather, it discerns the coherence of what God has done. Had God not done it, the transcendental method of *Rahner* would not be able to discourse about it all!

Rahner has continually protested that his "transcendental anthropology [is] not a rationalist and unhistorical merely formal deduction. It is a Rückführung or Rückgründung." That is, it is a "leading back to the ground of possibility of that which is already real and actual" (VIII, 52). Rahner has not been preoccupied with the question of method in theology. His own method has been developed in the act or performance of theologizing. His few explicit pages on method have usually been in response to objections which denounce his method as reductionist or idealist. Since these attacks do not seem to be declining, I have spent more pages of this book on Rahner's method than I would have preferred.

Rahner says that he does not object to the characterization of his theology as "transcendental" under two conditions. First, the term must be correctly understood, according to Rahner's own proper and particular use. Second, especially in view of its Kantian and Idealist connotations, the term must not be taken as an adequate description of the totality of his theology. Rahner insists that the term does not designate only an abstract, metaphysical or trans-mundane transcendence of the human being as spirit-subject. Rather, the human being is the subject of faith only and precisely as a historical essence with a concrete history. Transcendental reflection must show that the individual's own history as well as that of Jesus are significant for the individual person's salvation.

Human transcendence and human history are mutual. The one does not exist with the other; each exists only in the other. Human transcendence happens only in human history. This insight must be disclosed and emphasized by all theology in regard to a humanity which is already supernaturally graced by God's self-communication. For Rahner, theology is precisely transcendental when and because it asks

> the following question in regard to all the statements and propositions of faith and theology itself: How and why is the human being, in its very inmost essence, able to be the recipient to whom these propositions can and must be addressed? (XIV, 53).

That is, how is the human essence able to be the recipient of a salvation which happens in history, whose theological explanation is equally historical?

Like Simons and invoking Gerken, Scheffczyk refers to the events of salvation history as "purely *facta bruta* which are included in (Rahner's) system merely as material for transcendental experience." Were they merely material to be transcendentally experienced, his conclusion would be correct: "and thus they cannot be fully appreciated and valued in their magnificence ... insofar as they surpass merely human derivation and derivability." But he has it all backward. For Rahner it is the transcendental reflection (leading back) which reveals that these facts of salvation are precisely not brute. Their magnificence and surpassing ability to save the human being are discerned, not established, by the transcendental method. In the long run Rahner's transcendental method is a very elaborate expansion of the old scholastic axiom, "Whatever is received is received according to the mode of the receiver." Rahner's transcendental theology neither creates nor graces nor limits their possibility. Nor does it establish the possibility of such grace and creation in a world which has not yet been created and graced.

Nor does Rahner's method remove the possibility of surprise, by reducing the power and love of God to the present status of salvation history. His method shows only that the actual, really existing present status of humanity and Christianity is possible and meaningful both humanly and divinely. It does not exclude future surprise, for

> it states the fact that hope (in love) hopes that the real saving will of God is truly operative, that it operates by being hoped for as incalculable. God's salvific will acts by causing it to be hoped for precisely as what is the incalculable. Because the salvific will wills a salvation which is God himself, he has made a creature to attain it.[10]

Rahner's most persistent critic has probably been Hans Urs von Balthasar.[11] We have already seen his criticism of anonymous Christianity, which can justly be regarded as the consequence of the more fundamental criticism of Rahner's entire method. In this matter von Balthasar is not a latecomer. His methodological criticism dates to his 1939 review of Rahner's philosophical *Spirit in the World*. This was strongly reinforced by Gustave Siewerth's negative critique of the Marechal interpretation of St. Thomas Aquinas. His critique is more substantial than some of the relevance seeking pop criticism which surfaces from time to time.

Nevertheless, I do not understand why von Balthasar finds Rahner's approach so unacceptable. His own theology proceeds from a philosophical consideration of the beautiful as the innermost hallmark of transcendental being. To this "natural" beauty corresponds the "supernatural" glory or splendor (*kabod, doxa*) of biblical revelation and Christian theology. The principle of correlation is associated with Paul Tillich. One could easily show that this theological method is also found in Rahner and von Balthasar. In fact, one wonders how von Balthasar can theologically accomplish what he wants, unless he uses the transcendental method according to the special development Rahner has given it. This question becomes critical when one recalls that like Rahner, von Balthasar teaches (at least hopes for) the universal salvation of all humanity. Balthasar associates his conviction with Karl Barth's theology. This may give us a clue to his reluctance about Rahner's approach. There is in both Barth and von Balthasar a strong distrust of any self-sufficient philosophy. According to von Balthasar, "Theology can be done only in judgment of the human word by the divine word."[12] That is certainly true, and Rahner, as a Catholic theologian and believer has never taught otherwise. This statement may counter the transcendental theology of Hegel. It does not apply to Rahner's *method* of transcendental reflection. Hegel's key categories are knowledge and idea; Rahner's are faith and grace-revelation. Were Rahner Hegel, von Balthasar's critique would be fatal. But he is not, so it is not.

I am not sure that von Balthasar's critique is really pertinent. I say this not because I think Rahner has to be right but because I do not see how von Balthasar can reconcile his rejection of Rahner's approach with his own theological enterprise and salvation hopes. While some may find this section on von Balthasar unduly long, the climate in the Catholic Church as I write is such that his critique will become more and more influential. It will apply not only to Rahner, not only to other theologians, but to all aspects of Catholic Church life. Its intention is noble—to protect and enhance the unique grace and revelation of God in Jesus Christ. Its performance, however, is doubly questionable.

The first question is whether it actually reaches a real opponent or a straw man. Rahner would certainly not deny that

> in a genuine, personal self-communication and revelation . . . the only language possible between God and man is the Word of God. And then only if and insofar as God may be pleased to make himself understandable—that is, in the very act of speaking to man interpret His word to him.[13]

Rahner would not only not deny this but would also immediately begin to speak of the supernatural existential.

In the same vein, von Balthasar continues:

Thus it is clear why Karl Barth, in that he locates everything in God's word and its self-interpretation, rejects the *analogia entis*. However, it would be sufficient for his purposes, as it is for mine in this book, to reject the reduction (*Reduktion*) of revelation to a rational pre-understanding of God's existence, of the "divine." Whoever has never met a stranger, never talked with him and never been introduced to him, can indeed if he knows something of him, say that he "knows" him, but he can also equally well say that he does not know him.

German idealists may be guilty of such a reduction. Karl Rahner certainly is not. On September 5, 1980, von Balthasar received an honorary doctorate at The Catholic University of America. In his acceptance lecture he referred to the errors of transcendental theology. He mentioned Hegel, not Rahner.

He also favorably mentioned Rahner's theory that the world religions can be understood as a "seeking Christology" (XIII, 174, 225). This brings us to the second question. Without Rahner's general approach and without his theory of anonymous Christianity, can von Balthasar make such a favorable comment? Theologically, can von Balthasar reconcile his rejection of Rahner's transcendental reflection, supernatural existential, and anonymous Christianity with his own hope for universal salvation? Asked another way, how can he make the following statement without these three theological theories?

God, the wholly other than we, appears to us in the other, in the "sacrament of the brother." Indeed, only *as* the "wholly other" (than the world) is he at the same time the *not-other* (according to Cusa's, *De Non-aliud*). Only because he is over the world is he in it. But precisely as over, he retains the right, the power, the Word to reveal himself to us as everlasting love, to make himself understandable to us in his incomprehensibility, and precisely thus to give himself to us as gift.[14]

Rahner would certainly say, "Also my theology and life. Amen." His entire theological enterprise has been to show that God is not a stranger to his creation, where his creature, the human, is also the revelation and sacrament of this creating, gracing, saving God (XIV, 280). I find von Balthasar's criticism questionable because it does not actually reach Rahner and because it seems to gainsay von Balthasar's own theological effort.

The Knowledge Explosion and Theology

As preferable as I find Rahner's theology, I am as aware as he that his is not the only theology. By itself it is not sufficient to meet the needs of church and humankind in today's world. This is especially true because of the knowledge explosion. According to Rahner, this has made of us all theological *rudes*.[15] This term once described those uneducated people who could still legitimately believe, even though they could not intellectually account for all the grounds of credibility of their belief. Today even the most polished theologians must appear rough and rude, compared to the "universal person" of old. Hence, my criticism of von Balthasar's criticism is not meant to eliminate, but to contain. I think that such containment is especially critical because of the current conservatism in the Catholic Church. This conservatism is not without its own peculiar romantic pining for an earlier age when the unique glory of God shone forth more splendidly, perhaps even uniquely in Christian culture. Such a mentality may find von Balthasar's theology more appealing than Rahner's. That is fine. That it would find his critique of Rahner equally compelling would not be.

Other Objections

To find the criticism by Küng, Scheffczyk, and von Balthasar ineffective is not to assert that there are no problems in Rahner's theology. Some of these are more philosophical. For example, Thomists of the Gilson school object to Rahner's transcendental Thomism. Marechal's emphasis on the role of the mind's dynamism in grounding metaphysics is especially displeasing. Nor are they happy with his metaphysical theory of abstraction in the mind's pre-apprehension of being and God. However, as Gerald McCool has convincingly shown, Rahner is simply no longer, if ever, to be included in this philosophical school.[16] This does not mean that Rahner is right and these Thomists wrong. But it does mean that their criticism must be evaluated differently.

Of course, all pure phenomenologists, all empiricists, and all positivists can hardly be expected to be enthused by Rahner's metaphysical ontology. But, then, that is certainly their problem. And they can be immediately reminded of the aporiae of their own implicit metaphysics.

Continental transcendental Thomists as well as other theologians will not unreservedly accept what has been called Rahner's Hegelianism. Not all find Rahner's theology and ontology of the symbol immediately illuminating. The consequences for Rahner's theology of God as trinity and creator, for his Christology, ecclesiology, and sacramentology are obvious. Equally obvious, however, is the problematic of identifying Rahner as a Hegelian.

Some process theologians have desired to adopt Rahner into their family. Rahner's "dynamist" ontology of human knowing and being has some resemblance to certain process predilections. However, the inclusion of Rahner among process theologians would stretch the term beyond recognition. In any case, process theologians will generally find Rahner too much of a classical metaphysician.

In the final analysis, Rahner is his own man, his own theologian, indeed, his own theology. Whatever the influences of other thinkers, and they are clearly many and varied, he has gathered them all up and transformed them into his theology. He must stand and fall on his own achievement.

Lasting Difficulties

The most critical threat to Rahner's achievement is probably the validity of his distinction between transcendental and categorical. Of course, this is not a problem peculiar to him but is common to all philosophers and theologians. However, in Rahner's theology the pervasiveness of this distinction is especially visible and operative, so that he can less easily escape the consequences of a poor performance in regard to this matter.

In principle he has successfully defended himself against those who have accused him of ignoring the historical in favor of an abstract transcendental. This does not mean that in every instance his performance has been perfect, that he has preserved the perichoresis of the transcendental and the historical. In any case, it is often his opponents who do not keep the necessary balance. Whether deliberately or not, their solution tends to endow the historical with all the positive attributes traditionally reserved for the transcendental. Practically, this means that they can find eternal meaning and absolute value in the historical and the finite without establishing either the reality of this absolute eternal or its affirmative relationship to the finite historical. Rahner isn't guilty of this kind of false reasoning or reconciliation but is aware of the difficulty of reconciling history and transcendence. Even this awareness, however, does not mean that he always succeeds in actually reconciling them. He does not claim such success for himself. Neither should anyone else—for him or for anyone else.

The Scholastic Context

The problem above is universal, one with which every theologian has to contend. There are other problems which are limited. For Rahner one of these was the scholastic and neo-scholastic theology which was almost the official theology of the Catholic Church for years. One of Rahner's great achievements was freeing himself and his fellow theologians from imprisonment in this theology. However, this liberation itself placed a certain limitation on Rahner's own thought. The starting point for many of his writings is provided by this theology, to which he contrasts his own understanding. There is nothing wrong with this, since one has to start somewhere. However, people not familiar with this other theology may have initial difficulty understanding Rahner. Those who are not careful may falsely conclude that Rahner's theology is merely reactional and hence of value only to those who also need such a corrective. While knowledge of scholastic thought can be helpful in understanding Rahner, neither the intelligibility nor the value of his theology is dependent on it.

How Human Are Humans?

A more substantial problem for Rahner's theology is provided by the way human beings actually live their daily lives. Do they really respond to the everyday limitations they experience as transcendentally as Rahner's philosophy requires? Do they respond as brotherly to their neighbors in need as his theology requires? Are they as courageous in their daily lives? Do they really experience the Holy Spirit in all the moments of their lives and not in only a few isolated mystical moments? Does his book title *Everyday Faith* really describe their everydays? In these everydays do they really learn to let go of human *hybris* and to commend themselves into the hands of the Father-Mother God? I think so. I hope so. Nevertheless, I must also admit that the empirical evidence is not always all one would wish it to be. I am also aware that Rahner's own personal intensity must be factored into his theological theory.

Sacramental Frequency

How important this can be is illustrated by his position on the relationship between personal devotion and the frequency of sacramental celebration. Since one cannot always achieve a certain intensity of personal devotion, Rahner concludes that one can be satisfied with less frequent sacramental celebration. I would tend to travel from the other direction. Since one cannot always achieve a certain intensity of personal devotion, one needs sacramental celebration all the more. Ritual does not substitute for the personal but does support the personal, perhaps more so when the personal is flagging. Neither approach provides an arithmetic for the frequency of sacramental celebration and ritual worship. The topic illustrates the importance of Rahner's own personal religious experience for his theology. It also indicates why those of a cynical and skeptical bent might not be able to find Rahner's "mysticism of everyday living" in their daily lives.

Starting with the Christian

There is one more difficulty which could be the most serious threat to Rahner's mediation of the Christian tradition to the modern world. Not only his foes but even his friends describe him as "Starting with the Human," the title of Anne Carr's chapter in Leo O'Donovan's *A World of Grace: An Introduction to the Themes and Foundations of Karl Rahner's Theology*.[17] While such a description is not entirely wrong, neither is it right. He really starts with the Christian. This may be his greatest strength and, ultimately, could be his greatest weakness. Rahner's theology is truly and most intimately Christian. From its beginning to its heart to its end it is thoroughly Christian. The beginning of Rahner's theologizing is not the human experience. It is the Christian, the Christian tradition and Christian experience. It is the experience of God within this Christian tradition. On the basis of this tradition and experience Rahner finds that what could have been merely human is Christian, explicitly or anonymously.

Catholic Pantheism

In fact, because God has created precisely the world he has created, there never has been a merely "human" from which Rahner could have started. The world has always been graced, human being has always been Christian. So intense is the communion between God and humanity that Rahner has not shied away from speaking of a "Christian and Catholic pantheism which St. Paul already proclaimed in saying that in the end God is all in all."[18] The next development of consequence in Catholic theology will be the cultivation of this pantheism. Rahner's sacramental communion ontology will provide the stimulus for this development. This I consider to be Rahner's greatest significance for future theology. However, it could also be the source of the greatest obstacle to his effectiveness in the secular world. Secularists could claim that Rahner's thought is so caught up in Christianity that it begs the question of the human. They would be wrong, of course. Just as wrong as those who claim the opposite—that Rahner has begged the question of the divine. An unfortunate consequence of Rahner's superior theological mediation of the divine and the human is that advocates of the one or the other may misunderstand his synthesis. They may feel that either the divine or the human has come up short. In reality, they have come up together in the most intimate communion which God could create.

CHAPTER 5

Significance

What is Karl Rahner's significance? Is he friend or foe of the church and that church's God about whom he has written so much and whom he has wanted to serve? Is he merely a transitional theologian, with no serious lasting value and no significant future? This was often heard in the rebellious late sixties and early seventies. It is being heard again in the early conservative eighties.

In any case, Rahner's significance for the past and present is assured. He has certainly shepherded Catholic theology significantly. The Catholic Church reformed and redirected itself decisively in the Second Vatican Council, and without Rahner's person and theology the facts would have been different. Rahner's future significance is probably brighter than some fear and others hope. Any realistic prognosis must take von Balthasar's observation into consideration: "Nowadays who doesn't invoke Rahner for this or that, whenever it is a matter of the liberal expansion of dogma. If I have concerned myself with Rahner's ideas and words, it has been because they have been scattered abroad throughout the entire world."[1]

The peculiar development of his ideas has not always pleased Rahner or won his consent. But his theology has enabled younger theologians to be freed from what had become a strait jacket, the neoscholastic theology of official Catholic Church documents and seminary textbooks. Although this theology had never been given exclusive status in the Catholic Church, its influence was so pervasive in the West that it seemed to be official. Rahner showed that one could be a loyal Catholic thinker without ceding one's theological responsibility and creativity to this kind of pseudo-orthodoxy. To his great credit, he has always diligently distinguished his theology from a possible official church doctrine. Within the Roman Catholic tradition, the significance of this procedure can hardly be overestimated. Rahner has combined loyalty to his church and tradition with respon-

sible, creative innovation. At the same time his passionate advocacy
of his own ideas has not seduced him into identifying them with official church doctrine or into theologically excommunicating differing
ideas.

Pastoral and Systematic

Rahner's future significance is not limited to these general considerations. One of his greatest achievements is the perichoresis between
practical and theoretical theology. As Gerald McCool has noted,

> Rahner is a great *pastoral* theologian *precisely because* he is one
> of the greatest *systematic* theologians of this century. For
> Rahner, like Bonaventure and the great medievals, pastoral and
> spiritual theology are not something *added on to* a systematic
> theology . . . they are moments of the same *unified theological*
> activity from which systematic theology arises.[2]

They are a *sharing of experience* by the theologian and his dialogue
partner. Rahner has helped rescue theology from the irrelevance of
both academic integralism and the flight into commitment so
bemoaned by Wolfhart Pannenberg.[3] McCool has also correctly noted
the importance of experience and dialogue in the theological performance and product of Karl Rahner.

Ecumenism

Rahner has been ecumenically effective, not because he has been
an academic specialist in so-called ecumenical theology. Rather, he
has been able to retrieve the inner meaning of dogmas and doctrines
from the particular conceptual configurations in which they have
been encased. He has also been able to retrieve from the tradition
insights which have been forgotten or overlooked. The ecumenical
effect of this retrieval has been to expand both Catholic and Protes-
tant theological horizons. An added bonus of this expansion is the
increased capacity of the Christian religion to dialogue with the
greater world around it. For Rahner, ecumenical theology is not a
particular branch or kind of theology. It is, rather, simply theology
insofar as theology must face the future. This theology for the future
is the "necessary presupposition for the effective preaching of the
Gospel in the modern world such as it is" (X, 501).

It is most fitting that a Lutheran and an Anglican theologian should provide some of the finest testimonies to Rahner's significance. George Lindbeck asserts that Rahner is a "man who in comprehensiveness and sheer intellectual quality can, alone among contemporary Catholics, be ranged alongside of Barth and Tillich, and who in terms of balance is perhaps the greatest of the three." John Macquarrie says that

> Among contemporary theologians, I have found Karl Rahner the most helpful. . . . [He] is outstanding. He handles in a masterful way those tensions which constitute the peculiar dialectic of theology mentioned above: faith and reason, tradition and novelty, authority and freedom, and so on.[4]

Rahner's balance, noted by both of these theologians, has its source in what I would call his sacramental ontology. Its most direct development is in his articles on the Trinity, symbol, and sacraments. Its significance for Christology is clearly enormous. This sacramental understanding of being enables Rahner to avoid the extremes of chaos and monism. For him, being is neither totalitarian nor anarchic. It is, rather, unity in diversity and diversity in unity. Being is communion. In this communion various individual beings are not essentially at odds with one another. They are not essentially enemies or rivals. They are partners and friends. Individual beings make Being present and manifest in various ways. This ontology can—and must—be traced all the way back to God. The being of God is present and manifest in the Father, Son, and Holy Spirit. This makes clear that being is both communion and sacrament. It also makes clear that God can communicate and reveal himself in many and diverse manners (Hebrews 1:1-4). These ways and revelations are not contradictory but complementary.

Created being is not a threat to uncreated being. They can be and are positively related to one another. Likewise, nature and grace are meant for, not against each other. They are both communications of the divine communion to the non-godly. This ontology enables Rahner to avoid the monism of classical pantheism and some contemporary process theologies. It also enables him to avoid the abyss-ism of Barthian and similar theologies. Because of the divine initiative, human and divine being are truly partners. There has been, as the old

Roman liturgy exulted, an admirable commerce, a wondrous exchange. Because of this commerce, the human is simultaneously the communion of the non-godly with God and the sign or symbol of this communion. As the signful presence of God's saving will and action in the world, graced humanity is already God's sacrament (XIV, 280).

Creation, Christ, church are all to be understood on the basis of this sacramental, communion ontology. They are all the more or less intense presence and visibility of God in the non-godly. They are all the sensibly perceptible presence of the experience of God by the non-godly. Even Jesus, truly human and truly divine, can be understood this way, for all creation, of which he is the head, is the communion of God with the non-godly. Creation is therefore the expression of the experience of God by the non-godly. In Jesus this experience has reached its acme.

Sacraments in the customary sense are themselves the objectification of Jesus' own religious experience. He shared his own experience of God with his disciples in words and symbolic actions. Insofar as his disciples receive and pass on this shared experience, they become the church. The church and sacraments are possible because of the sacramental, communion ontology. They also reveal it. They also make it possible for us to understand how the Bible can truly be called the Word of God, revelation. In the words of the Bible the Word of God is truly communicated to us in a sensibly perceptible way. Even a doctrine like infallibility need not be a matter of such great consternation. It means that under certain conditions the communion of God and humanity in the truth achieves a certain sensibly perceptible visibility (X, 297).

All these individual sacraments must not make us lose sight of the most widespread sacrament. The very lives of Christians are themselves sacramental. They are the place where God's presence in the non-godly is experienced and expressed in a sensibly perceptible way. The temple is no longer a separate arena or building. Henceforth the true temple is the Body of Christ, and even this temple is not restricted to only certain parts of the world's population.

As we have seen, Rahner and even von Balthasar have spoken of the "sacrament of the brother." The perichoresis of love of God and love of humanity has revealed that Christ truly is present in even the unrecognized "least one" of our fellow human beings. The sacramental, communion ontology enables even "natural" creation to be the sacrament of God. The further intensity of grace enables this natural sacramental world to become truly the heavenly liturgy already here on earth. The history of the cosmos and the history of grace coincide (XIV, 233). The history of the world and the history of revelation also coincide. Why? How can this be? Because all being other than God is communion in God's being and the expression of the experience of this communion.

The Future Church

It seems to me that Rahner's theology will have a lasting significance because of this philosophical dimension. It enables him to be a properly systematic theologian as well as a profound thinker. Simultaneously, it is a limitation of his influence, since many either cannot or will not make the effort required for this philosophical journey.

The expansiveness which this philosophical dimension in general and sacramental communion ontology in particular give Rahner's theology is uniquely important for the present mission of the church. In the Second Vatican Council Rahner has discerned a decisive turning point in the history of the church.[5] He thinks that it has made a decision as significant as the early church's decision for the Gentile mission. In this new decision the church has become a truly universal church. It has therefore entered a third epoch. The first was Jewish Christianity; the second was Hellenistic Christianity and Western or European Christendom. This new epoch has only begun. The decision, although made, must be developed and made practical in the church's life and mission. Although Rahner's remarks immediately concern the Roman Catholic, he thinks that they apply equally to all Christian churches. If he is correct, the "fact" of Christianity will change significantly. It will no longer consist of Western Christianity exporting its theology, liturgy, and law to more or less colonial religious importers in the rest of the world. It will be a matter of each culture really and truly developing its own cultural expression of its own experience of God. This does not mean that Christ and the Christian church need be threatened or diminished. It does mean that the cultural sacramental expression of the ontological experience of God by the non-godly will become universally diverse, both within and without explicitly Christian communities. This requires not less theologizing but more, and not less rigorous but more so. The universal experience of God by God's creation must be discerned. Then the communion of the universality of this experience with the Christian experience and expression must also be explored. In this new phase of the *Glaubensnot* of humanity Rahner's theology alone will not be sufficient. However, it is clear that any and all biblical positivism will be utterly helpless in the face of this challenge. Only a philosophically rooted theology will have the necessary breadth of vision to see the unity of the many different historical sacraments of the experience of God in the one ontological communion of the non-godly with God. In the achievement of this vision Rahner alone, of course, will not be sufficient. But he will be paradigmatic.

Belief and the Eclipse of God

In the same vein Rahner has a special meaning for the contemporary individual believer. According to Martin Buber, we live in an age "when we (can) speak of an eclipse of God which is even now taking place."[6] Heidegger characterized this age similarly: "It is the time of the gods who have fled and the God who is coming. This is a dry season, because it consists of a twofold lack, a double nothing: the no longer of the fled gods and the not yet of the coming ones."[7] Rahner himself considers

> today's man to live in a world in which he experiences a certain thickness between himself and God. In a sense, this thickness closes man off from God. It consigns him to a closed world, a world of immeasurable size and diversity, beyond human powers to penetrate. Indeed, it is a world fully governed by its own independent profane constitutions and laws. Precisely as the world becomes steadily less divine, it also becomes less and less important and valuable (IV, 51).

In ancient Greece the philosopher Thales' world teemed with gods. The modern world teems with many things, but God does not seem to be one of them. Once the world seemed to be the monastery of God; for many it now seems to be but bare ruined choirs.

Is God really dead? And humanity, his image and likeness, a ruin?

Is Heidegger's pessimistic appraisal of human being correct—that it is toward and for the sake of death? Is the apeiron, that beyond, which is undeniably there, from which we come and to which we go, nothing? Sartre once said that "human life begins on the other side of despair."[8] The question is, of course, what is on the other side. Rahner once noted that there are "only two possible life styles: to be driven compulsively by the frustrations of anxiety or to embrace the cross, which is explicitly or implicitly the Cross of Christ" (VIII, 326). The "other side" determines which of these is properly human. Rahner's lasting significance is his ability to show that the "other side" of the world in which we live does make living in this world possible and meaningful. This world has been so created and graced that both in living our daily lives and dying our ordinary deaths we are able to share in Christ's cross-carrying and thus his resurrection. Because of the Christic character of all created being, death is not annihilation. It is the final letting go and thus the final fulfillment of faith and baptism. In faith, baptism, and finally death,

> the Christian allows himself to fall into the mystery we call God. He is convinced in faith and in hope that in falling into the incomprehensible and nameless mystery of God he is really falling into a blessed and forgiving mystery which divinizes us. He is also aware of this at the level of conscious reflection and explicit faith. Furthermore, he hopes for this blessed fall explicitly, not merely anonymously in the actual living of his daily life. In this sense to be Christian simply means to be truly human. But the Christian also knows that this life which he is living and of whose full-fillment he is aware can also take place there where one is neither explicitly Christian nor explicitly aware of being such.[9]

In Christ and Christianity both living and dying are revealed to be humanly possible because the apeiron is being-full.

Rahner's lasting significance? He has been able to show, even in a dry season, that this apeiron, the unlimited beyond, is not a dark and empty abyss, but the boundless mystery whom Jesus called "Abba, Father" (Mark 14:36).

Rahner has been able to help us understand that the darkness into which we creatures inevitably vesper is not the anguished night of nothing. It is the blessed night of Christmas.

How to Read Rahner

Beginners should start with the devotional or spiritual writings instead of the so-called academic, scientific, historical. Others should not neglect them. They reveal the true Rahner as well as and sometimes better than the scholarly writings. According to Rahner himself, they are all equally theological: "I think that I have done theology just as much in *The Eternal Year* as in the *Theological Investigations*" ("Brief," in Klaus Fischer, *Der Mensch als Geheimnis*. Freiburg: Herder, 1974, p. 403).

How can this be? Because theology reflects on one's own religious experience and religious tradition and then puts this reflection into words and sentences. There is always a double distance involved between the "thing" experienced and the experience; between the experience and its objectification in words and propositions. In principle this second distance is not greater in popular than in scholarly presentations. Furthermore, one's individual immediate experience never happens in a vacuum. It always takes place in a social, historical context. All theological reflection necessarily involves the individual and the tradition. The preceding pages have shown a remarkable perichoresis of individual experience and knowledge of the tradition in Rahner. For this reason one who reads the popular Rahner is not being deprived of the scholarly Rahner. Nor is he being served a thin gruel of pop piety instead of the rich banquet of theology. Popular means less difficult, not less scholarly. The difference is in the style and form, not in the theology.

All this having been said, I would recommend that the beginner start with *The Eternal Year*. Rahner himself mentions it explicitly in the above quotation, but there is a more compelling reason to start there. It is a kind of mini-systematic theology. As a series of meditations on the liturgical church year, it has to cover the whole range of Christian feasts. Its sixteen chapters ponder the major beliefs and insights of the Christian faith. It ranges from the cross of Good Friday to the laughter of Fastnacht, the German Mardi Gras (not Festnacht as the English translation has it). From the advent and Christmas birth of the Savior to the heavenly homecoming of him, his mother, and all the saints—to show the meaning of the truth revealed in these events is the aim of Rahner's little book. In addition, nowhere else can one better experience the intimacy of Rahner's language and thought.

Others have urged the reader to begin with two of Rahner's early books on prayer: *Encounters with Silence* and *On Prayer*. These are certainly typical and vintage Rahner. I wonder, though, whether their mood might not be a bit heavy—even lugubrious—for today's readers. Written shortly after World War II, they intensely reflect the mood of misery of those tragic years. From *The Eternal Year* I would move to *Mary Mother of the Lord* for two reasons. One is stated in the subtitle, "Theological Meditations." The other is more complicated. Rahner's "incarnational" theology demands that God's invisible grace achieve visibility in the real human world. The whole burden of his book on Mary is to show how this visibility happened in one particular case, Mary, the Mother of Jesus. Rahner shows how the doctrines and theology about Mary are really about the concrete form of God's grace in the real world. For those not familiar with the Catholic tradition of Marian devotion and doctrine this will be an added bonus. It will more than compensate for any initial difficulty they may have experienced because of their unfamiliarity.

I would then move on to *Ignatius of Loyola*. For an age which touts the value of narrative theology this book is especially pertinent. It is also a striking manifestation of how serious theology can be done in a non-scholarly form. Four collections of Rahner's popular writings would come next. In order of preference they are *Everyday Faith* and *Grace in Freedom*. Then *Opportunities for Faith* and *Christian at the Crossroads*. Here would be the fitting place for *The Shape of the Church to Come*. This book was occasioned by the National Synod of the Roman Catholic Bishops in Germany in 1971. It is a good example of how Rahner's theoretical systematic theology is also deeply pastoral. In this book he makes practical suggestions for revising the structures and practices of the church. By now one will certainly be able to read Rahner with greater speed and comprehension. Insights and expressions will have become familiar. Nevertheless, I would still continue with the devotional writings. I would next recommend *Meditations on the Sacraments,* with a caution about the introduction. From there I would go on to volumes 3, 7, 8 of the *Theological Investigations.* These also contain the special Rahnerian mixture of systematic, pastoral, and devotional writing.

By now even those who started at zero will know what Rahner is up to; they should have developed a good taste for the theology of Karl Rahner. From now on they should be able to do their own selecting from his *Investigations,* various encyclopedias, and other writings. Of course, not all of Rahner will be easy or even intelligible. Those without an adequate philosophical background will always be compromised in reading the more scholarly books and monographs.

Foundations

I would not go directly from the specific suggestions made above to the *Foundations.* The energy and knowledge required for the sustained reading of this book are considerable. Sustained, continuous reading is really the only proper way to read it. One would do well to spend time on the shorter scholarly articles in the *Investigations,* encyclopedias and monographs before tackling *Foundations.*

A few further cautions are also in order. *Foundations* is and is not a systematic summa. It is thoroughly systematic in that it is the application of Rahner's method of transcendental reflection to the major topics of theology. To some extent it can serve as a summa or summing up and summary of Rahner's theological insights. It is not, however, a systematic summa purely and simply—not even of Rahner's. So few pages could never contain an adequate systematic theology. Finally, it is not systematic in that all the necessary scriptural, traditional, and theological evidence and argument are not massed in support of the theory developed.

Rahner himself has noted certain deficiencies in regard to the Trinity (XIV, 48-62). However, he rejects all accusations or suspicions of modalism in regard to the Trinity, noting that even Cardinal Ratzinger could find no trace of it. He also concedes that the negativity of evil may have been misappreciated. He insists, however, that as a

Christian he finds emphasis on the hope of universal salvation altogether preferable to that theology which positively relates even eternal damnation to the glory of God. Angels and devils are simply
absent from the book. Whatever their theological value may be, it is
clearly not sufficient to warrant inclusion in this kind of book. He also
concedes a certain individualistic emphasis in the book, to the detri-
ment of the social and to the displeasure of political and liberation
theologians. Finally, he also admits a certain triumphalism in the section on the church. This is surprising since the sinful church has been
a constant theme in Rahner's theology from the very beginning. In
conclusion, Rahner exhorts his readers to accept his book as a positive, not exclusive statement of the faith.

Wherever one starts and however one proceeds, there is plenty of
Rahner to read. People sometimes wonder how he can write so much.
Doesn't he ever repeat himself? Yes. How can he have so many ideas?
He doesn't. He has only a few. He applies them vigorously and systematically to whatever topic an audience or the signs of the times
may propose. Isn't it an insult to say that such a learned and in-
sightful person has only a few ideas? No—that's considerably more
than most of us have.

Aids to Reading Rahner

I think the best guide to Rahner's works is the reading guide just
proposed. Along with the general introduction, it should equip one to
go to Rahner's writings themselves. There are two others I would
note here.

Anthologies of Rahner's writings are not easy to construct. An impressive one is by Gerald A. McCool, *A Rahner Reader* (New York:
Seabury, 1975). The only difficulty is, however, a considerable one. If
you can read and understand the selections in the *Reader,* you don't
really need a reader. You can read Rahner's works themselves. Mc-
Cool's general introductions to each selection are excellent.

There is another introduction to Rahner's thought which is keyed
to the order of *Foundations* and which gives specific readings accord-
ingly: Leo J. O'Donovan, ed. *A World of Grace* (New York: Seabury,
1980). I do not want to scare people from *Foundations.* However, my
experience has been that most people who are not specializing in the-

ology find it very difficult. I would, therefore, caution the reader not to think that O'Donovan's book will make reading *Foundations* easy. It is a good guide to Rahner's theology. But even a good guide cannot make a difficult journey easy.

Anthropocentric

Rahner's theology is frequently called anthropological and anthropocentric. He has accepted these designations, given the proper conditions. Some object to such an approach. They say it devalues God (or Christ) and overvalues humanity. However, as Rahner understands anthropocentric, it is not opposed to theocentric or Christocentric. It is opposed to cosmocentric. To understand this distinction we must examine the meaning of thought form.

Thought Form

"Thought form" is simply a transliteration of the German *Denkform*. This is a term from the theory of knowledge. It designates the source or principle of a particular way of thinking. Thought form has purely formal character. It does not refer primarily or directly to the objects of one's thought or the contents of one's thoughts about these objects. It does describe the precise manner or mode in which one thinks. It is the reason we think precisely as we do.

The easiest examples of what is meant are not the most pleasant. They involve various kinds of bigotry like racism and sexism. How often have we heard someone say, "They act like that because they are men or women, black or white, Polish or Italian, young or old." There is no end, of course, and the point will be made much better if you substitute the crude words of prejudice for the polite language I have used. However false these stereotypes are, they still illustrate the point at hand. The speaker thinks that there is some all-embracing principle which accounts for whatever the person in question does or thinks. That's what a thought form designates—the all-embracing starting point and source which "makes" our ideas to be exactly what and how they are. The thought form is operative whether we think of God or church, Loni Anderson or Boomer, peace or war, heaven or hell. There can be various kinds of thought forms—psychological, historical, cultural. We are interested in the most general. We could call it ontological. We are looking for an a priori pre-understanding of being in general, which would account for all our particular thoughts about being in general and all beings in particular.

Obviously this is a big order; and not an easy one. Discerning a thought form is always difficult. A thought form is not a clearly limited object or thing among many others. It is not like a basketball or book. The thought form does not have an independent existence of its own. Hence, it cannot be investigated head on, like laboratory objects in the natural sciences. A thought form can only be disclosed by use of the hermeneutic circle. Why? Because it exists only in the particular thoughts a given population thinks. It "in-forms" them, gives them their precise identity. We could say that the thought form and the thoughts form a circle. We have to get into the thoughts themselves to discover their principle, their source, their starting point.

Thoughts include ideas in their various objectifications and expressions. For our purpose the most important objectification is the word. But others are important too, like music, painting, sculpture, etc. By analyzing a given quantity of thoughts we can discover the thought form which gave rise to them. This presupposes, of course, that there is a homogeneous quantity which embodies a thought form. Through analysis we can find the "inspiration" of these individual cultural works. We can trace it throughout those individual works all the way back to its common origin and source. This principle is called the thought form.

Anthropocentric—Cosmocentric

More limited thought forms than the one we are seeking are, for example, the classical, the Greek, the scholastic, the romantic. Ours is the ontological. We are distinguishing the anthropocentric from the cosmocentric. This may well be the most important epochal change in the history of Western thought. It is referred to by some as the anthropocentric turn, by others as the Copernican turn. The latter is a play on Copernicus' heliocentric theory. According to this theory the sun, not the cosmos is the center around which everything revolves. In the anthropocentric thought form, not the cosmos but the anthropos (man) is the starting point whence flow all particular ideas.

In the cosmocentric thought form all thinking begins with the cosmos—material, space occupying, sensibly perceptible being. The really real is this cosmos. All other beings are modifications of it. Humanity as the starting point means that all thinking begins with the human subject, not the cosmic object. Hence, the really real is knowing, loving, choosing, being free, being uniquely once-for-all. This is true being. All other beings are to be measured against this subject being.

Whether this turning point in history is called anthropocentric or Copernican, it marks the moment when the human being's thought and reflection turned from the external cosmos around him or her to human self. We are all familiar with the classical axiom that the proper study of humanity is humanity. The anthropocentric turn emphasizes this. Humans are not the only proper object of human thinking. They are also the source of categories of thinking. It is possible, then, for theology, ontology, and cosmology to begin in anthropology. This can also be done in Christianity, which still insists that God and Christ are more being-full than humans.

Immediately we should point out that one of these is not right, the other wrong. Both can mediate truth. Each has advantages and disadvantages. The disadvantage of the cosmocentric approach is that it can easily regard the human being as just one more homogeneous part of the universe. It underestimates the dignity of the free, human person. The disadvantage of the anthropocentric is that it easily forgets the human's location within a pre-given objective universe. It underestimates cosmic corporeality and consequent equality with other creatures. The human being easily becomes absolute subject, total freedom.

Examples

Some examples applying this distinction may help illuminate it and at the same time illustrate its importance. We shall begin with conscience. In the cosmocentric universe of the ancient Greeks Oedipus is "guilty" of patricide, even though he has not the faintest inkling of the crime he (is supposed to have) committed. The human being is so much a part of the cosmos that even though Oedipus was not aware that the man he had slain was his Father and the woman he had wed his Mother, he was still guilty of having destroyed the order of the cosmos. For this crime retribution must be exacted. There is no room for what we call conscience. In the absolute anthropocentrism of some modern philosophies and theologies the only norm is the individual human being. Crude expressions are "Do your own thing" or "If it feels good, do it." Hardly more sophisticated expressions can be found in the situation ethics of Joseph Fletcher and his disciples. The situation is really rigged so that one can hardly decide anything but the most loving thing. That, of course, is not the solution—it is the problem. For this kind of anthropocentrism, being and the human being's situation and decision simply coincide. There is no room for conscience here either.

Rahner's moderate anthropocentrism is well represented by Thomas Aquinas' doctrine of the erroneous conscience. According to this, the human being must follow his conscience even when it is erroneous. Aquinas was the first to establish this theologically. Note the middle way between the extremes of cosmocentrism and absolute anthropocentrism. The conscience is indeed the ultimate arbiter of human choice, but it is not the ultimate norm of morality. For the human being really is in the pre-given cosmic universe, although not homogeneously. The human being is never merely object, not even primarily. The human is primarily subject, but always in the cosmos. Humanity's unsurpassability is within, not outside the cosmic universe. In the anthropocentric thought form human dignity is revealed more strikingly than in the cosmocentric. It must also be conceded that determining the moral duties and responsibilities in the anthropocentric thought form is more difficult. This difficulty has two chief causes. The first is the greater emphasis on the uniqueness of each person. The second is an inevitable consequence of the first. Morality is located much more emphatically in human relationships than in cosmic, physical objects. Further development of this factor is not possible here. It is too important, however, to go unmentioned.

Among other examples of anthropocentric-cosmocentric contrast the following suggest themselves immediately. In a cosmocentric understanding of revelation emphasis tends to be on the objects revealed. Objects here would include the means, words and sentences, as well as the topics, the doctrines. In the anthropocentric understanding revelation would be seen as the deepening and intensifying of the consciousness, so that the truth-horizon would be expanded. Cosmocentrically grace is thought of as a thing—something poured into the container of the soul. Thus we have often spoken of the infusion of grace. Anthropocentrically grace is conceptualized as a relationship of friendship between humans and God. Grace is their mutual encounter and presence. Finally, from St. Thomas comes an interesting discussion of what makes a human being a human. Early in his career he noted that "the soul (= human being) has its being (esse) more truly where it loves (amat) than where it [merely] is (est)" (1 Sent. 15, 5, 3 ad 2). This means that to be human is primarily to love, not merely just to be. This is much closer to Rahner's definition of the human being as *Spirit in the World* than the Aristotelian and Scholastic "rational animal."

Again I hasten to caution that both thought forms are correct. But one is, if it may be permitted, more correct. The anthropocentric puts the emphasis on the precisely human, on what distinguishes the human being from merely animal, vegetable, mineral. There is a price to be paid of course. The cosmocentric usually seems to be more definite, easier to get hold of. The anthropocentric seems to be more evasive; it eludes one's grasp. Revelation as a collection of words and sentences is easier to deal with than an expanded horizon of human consciousness. Rational animal is easier to locate than the truly free, knowing performance of the human subject. Once understood, however, the anthropocentric does seem to provide more human meaning than the cosmocentric approach.

At times both younger and older students of theology will have difficulty with Rahner's anthropocentric approach. In *Christliche Anthropozentrik* (Munich: Kosel, 1962), his best and by far most relevant book, J.B. Metz showed that the anthropocentric thought form is already discernable in St. Thomas Aquinas. Customarily, however, its beginning is located in Luther, Descartes, or Kant. In any case, the modern person's mode of thinking is anthropocentric. Because of its emphasis on the human subject, it is suspected of being subjectivistic. Although it can tend toward subjectivism, it does not have to. It need not reduce all being to the level of the human subject. I emphasize again—the anthropocentric thought form does not make the human being either the only or the highest being. It does take its categories for explaining being—whatever and however being might be—from the precisely human. Its explanation starts from the human. In any case, subjectivism would be no worse than objectivism.

Whether anthropocentric or cosmocentric might be more meaningful in itself is one question. However, today's theologians have little choice if they want to make the Christian revelation and tradition accessible to

> the man of today and tomorrow who has truly become subject, who is delivered over to and responsible to himself, not only theoretically, but also practically. He has made the Copernican turn from cosmocentric to anthropocentric, not only conceptually and religiously, but also practically (VI, 20).

Karl Rahner's theology is thoroughly anthropocentric. This does not mean that he puts humanity in the middle instead of God or Christ. It means, rather, that when he tries to explain God and Christ, humans and the world, his starting point is the category of the anthropos. His basic concepts are the precisely human categories of freedom, knowing, love, choice, uniqueness. The human is not the means whereby Rahner displaces and replaces God. It is the means whereby he understands and worships God and shares this with other humans.

Finally, anthropocentricism does have a privileged recommendation. When God decided to explain himself to the cosmos, he did, after all, become human. In Christ the world has certainly and unsurpassably become not only Christo—but also anthropocentric.

Special Terms

Anthropocentric-cosmocentric. See appendix II.

Being. This word can be used in two ways. It can be the most universal word. In this way it simply designates the minimum—anything that exists at all. Or, negatively, it designates anything that does not not exist. The second way in which this word is used is neither universal nor minimal. In this usage it designates the fullness of being—being that is free, knows, loves, and chooses. Each usage is legitimate. Each has advantages and disadvantages. The only reliable advice that can be given to the reader is to be alert.

Categorical. This word is usually distinguished from and contrasted with transcendental. It designates a being or manner of being which is limited, historical, particular, concrete. In Rahner's thought it designates especially the specific or definite content of everyday acts of knowing and choosing. It is in contrast to the transcendental openness to and dynamism toward being in general.

Existential. This word designates those precisely distinguishing characteristics or dimensions of human being as such by which human being is human and not something else.

Existentiell. This word emphasizes the very concrete, definite, peculiar circumstances of any given, particular human being (or group of human beings as distinct from another group). What makes me me and not somebody else is existentiell.

Hypostatic Union. This technical term comes from Greek philosophy. It was used by Christian theologians to describe the being of Jesus. Its classical expression is that in Jesus there is one person (divine) and two natures (human and divine). This term is correct, but not easily understood today. Its intention remains most important for us today—to preserve the full and perfect union of the divine and human in Jesus.

Ignatian. This word comes from the name of St. Ignatius of Loyola, who founded a religious order known as the Society of Jesus. Ignatian is the adjective which describes things characteristic of this saint and also of the religious order he founded.

Jesuit. This adjective designates members of or things pertaining to the religious order founded by St. Ignatius of Loyola. Sometimes Ignatian and Jesuit are used interchangeably; for example, Jesuit or Ignatian spirituality. Here caution is due.

Ontological. This word designates the mode of thinking about reality in which particular concepts or ideas have their source in the precisely human experience of personal knowing and choosing. See anthropocentric. It is sometimes also used as a synonym for metaphysical. Then it means the highest level of human thinking which extends to all beings insofar as they "be" at all.

Non-godly. I have used this term to designate anything that really is, but is not simply God himself. It applies to whatever is created, both the human and the cosmic. It has no negative moral overtones.

Transcendence. This word means basically going beyond any limit or boundary. In God it means being simply beyond the limitations of anything finite. In humans it means the dynamism of the human spirit which always moves beyond any given limit or particular being to the infinite horizon which makes the human being's individual acts possible and coherent.

Transcendental. In Rahner's thought this term designates human experience insofar as individual, definite acts involve the implicit unthematic awareness of being in general. This wholeness or fullness of being in general is what makes these individual acts possible. It cannot be the direct object of thought the way things are.

Supernatural Existential. This is Rahner's term to designate the effect of God's universal saving will on the world he created. It means that the world is graced before any human response to God is made.

It means that real, de facto human history has never been merely natural. It has always been super-natural—in the state of grace. Hence, in this real world in which we live one existential of being human is grace.

Thematic-Unthematic.   This pair is similar to explicit/implicit. Thematic designates something which is present, and one is aware of it. It is an explicit theme of one's consciousness, it is present thought. Unthematic means that something is already present in one's consciousness, but one has not yet made an explicit theme of it.

Bibliography

Titles actually used in this book, as well as a few others especially apt for this book's intended readers, are included.

CROSSROAD

In the United States most of Rahner's books are now published by Crossroad, which acquired its copyright from Helicon and Herder and Herder and most recently Seabury. *Theological Investigations,* volumes 1-16, 1961-1979. In late 1980 volume 15 was still unavailable. Until volume 7 the numbering of the original German and the English translations were the same. Beginning with volume 7 of the original German, the English translation has divided each German volume into two. The original German, *Schriften zur Theologie,* 1-14, have all been published by Benziger of Einsieldeln, Switzerland, 1954-1980.

Other Books

The Christian Commitment, 1963.
The Church and the Sacraments, 1963. (Now reprinted by Burns and Oates in London).
The Dynamic Element in the Church, 1964.
Revelation and Tradition, 1966.
Spirit in the World, 1968.
Everyday Faith, 1968.
Hearers of the Word, 1969.
Grace in Freedom, 1969.
The Trinity, 1970.
Opportunities for Faith, 1970.
On the Theology of Death, 1973.
The Shape of the Church to Come, 1974.
Christian at the Crossroads, 1975.
Meditations on Freedom and the Spirit, 1977.
Meditations on the Sacraments, 1977.
Foundations of Christian Faith, 1978.

The Spirit in the Church, 1979.

Encyclopedias, Dictionaries

Encyclopedia of Theology: The Concise Sacramentum Mundi, 1975.
Sacramentum Mundi, I-VI, 1970.
Theological Dictionary, 1965.

Other Publishers

On Prayer. New York: Paulist, 1958.
Encounters with Silence. New York: Paulist, 1960.
The Eternal Year. Baltimore: Helicon, 1964. This is now available
    from Westminster, MD: Christian Classics.
Do You Believe in God? New York: Paulist, 1969.
Ignatius of Loyola. London: Collins, 1979.

Secondary Literature

There is a flood of publications about Karl Rahner's thought. I
shall mention only three here. They are mentioned because of their
emphasis on the mystical dimension of Rahner's theology.

Klaus P. Fischer, *Der Mensch als Geheimnis. Die Anthropologie Karl
    Rahners* (Freiburg: Herder, 1974). This is a long (420 pages) and
    wide-ranging examination of Rahner's thought and style of think-
    ing. I include it although it is in German, because I think it is the
    best extensive introduction. Furthermore, the German is not all
    that difficult.

Harvey D. Egan, *The Spiritual Exercises and the Ignatian Mystical
    Tradition* (St. Louis: The Institute of Jesuit Sources, St. Louis Uni-
    versity, 1976). This is not directly a book about Rahner. However,
    since it is a revision of the author's doctoral dissertation directed
    by Rahner, it does mediate Rahnerian insights.

Michael J. Walsh, *The Heart of Christ in the Writings of Karl Rahner*
    (Rome: Pontifical Gregorian University, Analecta Gregorianna,
    1977). This is also a doctoral dissertation. It uses the traditional
    Devotion to the Sacred Heart, especially dear to Jesuits, to ex-
    amine Rahner's theology in regard to the priority of religious ex-
    perience and the mutual relationships among theology, spirituality
    and anthropology.

Notes

Chapter 1

1. Herbert Vorgrimler, *Karl Rahner* (New York: Paulist, 1966) p.21. The English translation has Honecker.
2. Karl Rahner, *Spirit in the World* (New York: Seabury, 1968).
3. In order to keep the footnotes to a minimum, I shall include the reference in the text where this is possible. All translations from titles given in German are my own. References to the *Schriften* will be given in the text, a Roman numeral for the volume, Arabic for the page. In some other cases only a shortened title with page number will be given. Complete information is in the bibliography.
4. *Worte ins Schweigen* (Innsbruck: Rauch, 1947), p. 29. Likewise, in *Schriften III*, (p. 463), Rahner speaks of the knowledge humans have of God as one "in which we do not seize, but are seized."
5. See Karl Lehmann, "Karl Rahner," in Herbert Vorgrimler and Robert Vander Gucht, eds., *Bilanz der Theologie im 20. Jahrhundert: Bahnbrechende Theologen* (Freiburg: Herder, 1970), pp. 149-162. Vorgrimler, op. cit., p. 28.
6. This interview first appeared in the *Herder-Korrespondenz* in February, 1974. It has since been published in a collection of Rahner's writings titled *Herausforderung des Christen* (Freiburg: Herder, 1975). It is an excellent compact summary of Rahner's thought in his own words.
7. Rahner's statement is included in a report by Robert Delaney in *The National Catholic Reporter*, Nov. 23, 1979, p. 1. Rahner's concern is continued in a protest about certain Catholic Church bureaucratic procedures used against theologians whose orthodoxy is suspect: "Theologie und Lehramt," *Stimmen der Zeit*, 105 (1980), pp. 363-375.
8. See Karl H. Neufeld and Roman Bleistein, *Rahner-Register* (Einsiedeln: Benziger, 1974), pp. 181-183.
9. Ralph Wiltgen, *The Rhine Flows into the Tiber: The Unknown Council* (New York: Hawthorne, 1966), pp. 19, 95.
10. In an interview with Leo O'Donovan, entitled "Living into Mystery: Karl Rahner's Reflections at 75," *America* 140 (March 10, 1979), pp. 179-180.
11. See Vorgrimler, *Karl Rahner*, p. 51; Lehmann, *Karl Rahner*, p. 148.
12. Karl Rahner, "Selbstporträt," in W. Ernst Böhm, ed., *Forscher und Gelehrte* (Stuttgart: Battenberg, 1966), p. 21.

13. "Karl Rahner," *Bilanz*, p. 148.
14. "Selbstporträt," p. 21.
15. Bettschart's own words ("so schweres Zeug"—"schwer" means both heavy and difficult), cited by R. Bleistein, *Rahner-Register*, p.14.
16. Karl G. Steck, *Theologische Rundschau* 35 (1970), p. 174.
17. "Living into Mystery," p. 177.
18. "Selbstporträt," p. 21.

Chapter 2

 1. Patrick Granfield, *Theologians at Work*, (New York: Macmillan, 1967), p. 43.
 2. Karl Rahner, "Replik. Bemerkungen zu: Hans Küng, Im Interesse der Sache," *Zum Problem Unfehlbarkeit* (Freiburg: Herder, 1971), p. 66.
 3. Karl Rahner, "Ein Brief von P. Karl Rahner," in Klaus Fischer, *Der Mensch als Geheimnis* (Freiburg: Herder, 1974), p. 409.
 4. Karl Rahner, Eberhard Simons, *Zur Lage der Theologie* (Düsseldorf: Patmos, 1969), pp. 35, 36.
 5. The difference between Rahner and Kant in regard to the transcendental method is neatly presented by Francis Fiorenza, "Introduction," in Karl Rahner, *Spirit in the World* (New York: Herder & Herder, 1968), pp. xix-xlvii.
 6. Karl Rahner, *Foundations of Christian Faith* (New York: Seabury, 1978), p. 33. The original German is considerably more forceful: "denn das Nichts begründet nichts." *Grundkurs des Glaubens* (Freiburg: Herder, 1976), p. 44.
 7. Gerald McCool, *A Rahner Reader* (New York: Seabury, 1975), p. xxviii.
 8. William Richardson, *Heidegger: Through Phenomenology to Thought* (The Hague: M. Nijhoff, 1963), p. 49. I am aware of the danger involved in terming "existential" a category. Heidegger himself uses "existential" to designate the essential components of the structure of There-being as existence. He restricts *Kategorie* to the structural determination of beings other than There-being. However, I take the risk, for the sake of an important point I want to make. Rahner has been able to go beyond the customary philosophical *categories* (for example, Aristotelian) operative in Catholic theologizing and adapt or find new ones. Thus, he is able to make the Catholic tradition of the "deposit of faith" available to modern readers in our own language, on our own grounds. Heidegger has been a bountiful source of such "categories" for Rahner.
 9. See George Muschalek, "Natürlichkeit und Menschlichkeit" in Herbert Vorgrimler, ed., *Gott in Welt: Festgabe für Karl Rahner*, vol. II (Freiburg: Herder, 1964), pp. 103-112.
10. Karl Rahner, *Hörer des Wortes*, revised edition by John B. Metz (Munich: Kosel, 1963), pp. 142, 22.
11. *Herausforderung*, p. 135.

12. Otto Hentz, "The Idea of Christianity," *Thought* (December 1978), p. 440.

13. See my "Karl Rahner and the Christian Philosophy of St. Thomas Aquinas," in William Kelly, ed., *Karl Rahner: Discoverer in Theology* (Milwaukee: Marquette University Press, 1980).

14. Karl Rahner, *Trinity* (New York: Seabury), p. 11.

15. Karl Rahner and Herbert Vorgrimler, *Theological Dictionary* (New York: Seabury, 1965), p. 115.

16. Although Rahner has surrendered this idea of late (XII, 461), I still think that there is something fundamentally important and inamissible about it for an incarnational and creational ontology and theology which want to be and must remain anti-gnostic. For details on this point, see Klaus Fischer, "Der Tod—Trennung von Seele und Leib," in Herbert Vorgrimler, ed. *Wagnis Theologie* (Freiburg: Herder, 1979), pp. 328-335, and H. Vorgrimler, *Der Tod im Denken und Leben des Christen* (Dusseldorf: Patmos, 1978), p. 115ff.

17. J. B. Metz, *Glaube in Geschichte und Gegenwart*, (Mainz: Grunewald, 1977), pp. 62, 125.

18. *Herausforderung*, p. 137.

19. "Warum uns das Beten nottut," *Lechtturm* 18 (1924-25), pp. 310-11.

20. Karl Rahner, *Worte ins Schweigen* (Innsbruck: Rauch, 1954; first published in 1947), p. 29.

21. Karl Rahner, *Chancen des Glaubens* (Freiburg: Herder, 1971), p. 90.

22. See Hans Küng, *On Being a Christian* (Garden City: Doubleday, 1976), pp. 89-110, especially pp. 97-100. Hans Urs von Balthasar, *The Moment of Christian Witness* (New York: Newman, 1968), pp. 47-78. An excellent placing of Rahner's anonymous Christian theory in the context of his entire theology is provided by Klaus Riesenhuber as the "Afterword" to Anita Roper's *The Anonymous Christian* (New York: Sheed & Ward, 1966).

23. Ernst Jüngel, "Extra Christum nulla salus—als Grundsatz natürlicher Theologie," in Elmar Klinger, ed., *Christentum innerhalb und ausserhalb der Kirche* (Freiburg: Herder, 1976), p. 122.

24. Jungel, p. 135. Hans Küng, "Anonyme Christen-wozu?" in *Orientierung*, 39 (1975), p. 215. There is a condensation of this and two other articles by H. R. Schlette and Rahner in response to it in *Theology Digest*, 1976.

25. See Karl H. Weger, *Karl Rahner* (Freiburg: Herderbücherei, 1978), p. 105.

26. *Schriften*, XII, p. 276. And thus is calmly undone Hans Küng's question, intended to be an insuperable argumentum ad hominem: "And what would Christians say if they were graciously recognized by Buddhists as 'anonymous Buddhists'?" See his *On Being a Christian*, p. 98.

27. In *Herder-Korrespondenz*, 76 (1976), p. 76.

28. Hans Urs von Balthasar, *Science, Religion and Christianity* (London: Burns and Oates, 1958), p. 148.
29. Hans Urs von Balthasar, *Cordula* (Einsiedeln: Johannes, 1966), pp. 128-129. This appendix to the third German edition is not included in the English translation. The reference is to Henri de Lubac, "*Paradoxe et Mystere de l'Eglise* (Paris: Aubier, 1967), pp. 120-163.
30. Jess Stein, ed., *The Random House Dictionary of the English Language*, unabridged edition (New York: Random House, 1973), p. 61.
31. Karl Rahner, *Grundkurs des Glaubens* (Freiburg: Herder, 1976), p. 309.
32. Cited by Hugo Rahner, *Our Lady and the Church* (New York: Pantheon, 1960), p. 14.

Chapter 3

1. J. B. Metz, "Widmung und Würdigung," in Herbert Vorgrimler, ed., *Gott in Welt I* (Freiburg: Herder, 1964), p. 5.
2. "Eucharisticon Fraternitatis," in *Gott in Welt II*, p. 895.
3. Karl Lehmann, "Karl Rahner," in Herbert Vorgrimler and Robert Vander Gucht, eds., *Bilanz der Theologie im 20. Jahrhundert* IV (Freiburg: Herder, 1970), p. 170.
4. Gerald McCool, "Karl Rahner and the Christian Philosophy of St. Thomas Aquinas," in William Kelly, ed., *Karl Rahner: Discoverer in Theology* (Milwaukee: Marquette University Press, 1980).
5. In *Theological Studies*, 38 (Sept. 1977), pp. 555-556. Karl Rahner and Wilhelm Thüsing, *A New Christology* (New York: Seabury, 1980). Unfortunately, the English translation is not the book one would expect. The title itself is misleading. *A New Christology* does not translate *Christologie—Systematisch und Exegetisch*. The content is even more so. The section by Rahner is not at all the same in the translation as in the original German. In fine print on the copyright page we read both "originally published as *Exegetisch* 1972" and then "adapted by Karl Rahner. New material copyright 1980." The omission of the original Rahner material is unfortunate because it is an extended, sustained development (sixty pages) and defense of his transcendental Christology. It is keyed to the current discussions of Scripture about Christologies from above and below and was part of a course on Christology which Rahner team-taught with the exegete, Wilhelm Thüsing. In his part of the original book, Thüsing referred regularly to Rahner's part. There was something of a real dialogue between the systematic theologian and the biblical scholar. All that is lost in the English version. Consequently the point that Harvey Egan makes in the review just cited is also lost.
6. Francis Fiorenza, "Rahner's Ecclesiology," in L. Salm, ed. *CTSA Proceedings 1978* (Mahwah, N.J.: Darlington Seminary, 1979), pp. 229-254.
7. Leo Bakker, *Freiheit und Erfahrung* (Würzburg: Echter, 1970).

8. George Lindbeck, *The Future of Roman Catholic Theology* (Philadelphia: Fortress, 1970), p. 10.
9. A. Carr, *The Theological Method of Karl Rahner* (Missoula: Scholars Press, 1977; a 1971 Ph.D. dissertation), pp. 5, 257.
10. Karl Rahner, *The Dynamic Element in the Church* (New York: Seabury, 1964), p. 155. The essay quoted was first published in 1956.
11. *The Spirit in the Church* (New York: Seabury, 1979), pp. 1-32. *Meditations on Freedom and the Spirit* (New York: Seabury, 1978), pp. 7-32.
12. Karl Rahner, *Glaube, der die Erde liebt* (Freiburg: Herder, 1966), pp. 152-153.
13. *Worte ins Schweigen*, p. 29.
14. Karl Rahner, *Wagnis des Christen* (Freiburg: Herder, 1974), p. 23. On p. 17 of the English translation, *Christian at the Crossroads* (New York: Seabury, 1975), we read *inconceivability* instead of *incomprehensibility*. This is not only an inexact translation but is also misleading. Pushed to its logical conclusion, it would be heresy. Both the context and the vocabulary emphasize that although God is knowable (conceivable), this knowledge is not exhaustive or comprehensive. Elsewhere the translator correctly rendered *Unbegreiflichkeit* as *incomprehensibility*. The present gaffe is therefore all the more puzzling. This recalls another mistranslation in Rahner's career when in 1966 he was denounced by the Vatican newspaper *L'Osservatore Romano* for having spoken of "God's unknowability." Then he had also spoken of "God's incomprehensibility." One is heresy, the other is true doctrine, and the distinction is worth attending to. The account is in *The New World* (Chicago), June 3, 1966, p. 1.
15. Leo J. O'Donovan, "Living into Mystery," *America* March 10, 1979, p. 178.
16. Karl Rahner, "Foreword," in L. Roberts, *The Achievement of Karl Rahner* (New York: Herder and Herder, 1967), p. viii.
17. R. Wisser, ed., *Martin Heidegger im Gespräch* (Freiburg: Herder, 1970), p. 48.
18. Karl Rahner, *Gnade als Freiheit* (Freiburg: Herder, 1968), pp. 266, 270.

Chapter 4

1. Hans Urs von Balthasar, *Cordula* (Einsiedeln: Johannes, 1966, 3rd edition), p. 125.
2. For example, Juan Segundo, *The Liberation of Theology* (Maryknoll: Orbis, 1976), pp. 89-182, especially pp. 89, 112. Rahner, *Schriften*, X, 13.
3. See Andrew Tallon, "Getting to the Heart of the Matter: Spirit," *Louvain Studies*, vol. 11 (Spring 1969), pp. 277-282.
4. E. Simons, *Philosophie der Offenbarung* (Stuttgart: Kohlhammer, 1966), p. 125.

5. James Mackey, *New Catholic World*, July, 1978, pp. 75-80.
6. *Nichomachean Ethics*, I, 3 (1094 b 12-14).
7. Karl Rahner, *Herausforderung des Christen* (Freiburg: Herder, 1975), p. 137.
8. Hans Küng, "Toward a New Consensus in Catholic (and Ecumenical) Theology," *Journal of Ecumenical Studies* 17 (1980), p. 2.
9. Leo Scheffczyk, "Christentum als Unmittelbarkeit zu Gott," *Internationale Katholische Zeitschrift Communio* 6 (1977), pp. 444-450.
10. Karl Rahner, "Salvation," *Enclopedia of Theology*, p. 1504.
11. The sharpest critique is in his *The Moment of Christian Witness* (New York: Paulist Newman, 1969). This is a translation of *Cordula*, but without the "afterword" to the third German edition in which von Balthasar defends his attack on Rahner, especially the theories of the supernatural existential and anonymous Christianity, but also on the transcendental method and the Marechal-Rahnerian interpretation of St. Thomas.
12. Hans Urs von Balthasar, "Der Ort der Theologie," *Verbum Caro* (Einsiedeln: Johannes, 1960), p. 166.
13. Hans Urs von Balthasar, *Glaubhaft ist nur Liebe* (Einsiedeln: Johannes, 1966), p.30.
14. *Glaubhaft*, p. 100. The inadequacy of von Balthasar's own explanation is unintentionally exposed in the laudatory dissertation of Giovanni Marchesi, *La Christologia di Hans Urs von Balthasar* (Rome: Gregorian University Press, 1977), especially p. 394.
15. Karl Rahner, *Foundations of Christian Faith* (New York: Seabury, 1978), p. 9.
16. Gerald McCool, "Karl Rahner and the Christian Philosophy of St. Thomas Aquinas," in William Kelly, ed., *Karl Rahner: Discoverer in Theology* (Milwaukee: Marquette University Press, 1980).
17. (New York: Seabury, 1980), p. 17.
18. Karl Rahner, *Eventus et Mediatio Salutis*, II, 18. This is a set of mimeographed notes reproducing a series of lectures Rahner gave in the late 1960s in Rome and is strictly unofficial. Although the copy was not edited or checked by Rahner himself, this does not detract from its value. It does, however, advise caution in its use.

Chapter 5

1. Hans Urs von Balthasar, *Cordula* (Einsiedeln: Johannes, 1966), p. 126.
2. Gerald McCool, "Introduction" in his *A Rahner Reader* (New York: Seabury, 1975), pp. xxiv, xxv.
3. See Wolfhart Pannenberg, *Theology and the Philosophy of Science* (Philadelphia: Westminster, 1973), p. 76, referring to W. Bartley's *Retreat to Commitment*, 1962.
4. George Lindbeck, "The Thought of Karl Rahner," *Christianity and*

Crisis, 25 (October 18, 1965), pp. 211-215. John Macquarrie, *Principles of Christian Theology* (New York: Scribners, 1977, 2nd ed.), p. vii.

5. Karl Rahner, "A Basic Interpretation of Vatican II," *Theological Studies* 40 (1979), pp. 716-727.
6. Martin Buber, *Eclipse of God* (New York: Harper, 1957), p. 127.
7. Martin Heidegger, *Erläuterungen zu Hölderlins Dichtung* (Frankfurt: Klosterman, 1963, 3rd ed.), p. 116.
8. Jean-Paul Sartre, *Les Mouches* (Paris: Gallimard, 1947), p. 114.
9. Karl Rahner, *Grundkurs des Glaubens* (Freiburg: Herder, 1976), p. 413. See also *Schriften*, XII, pp. 316, 290, 300, 308, and *Everyday Faith* (New York: Herder and Herder, 1967), p. 186.

Index